Democracy

Michael Frayn was born in London in 1933 and read Russian, French and Moral Sciences (Philosophy) at Emmanuel College, Cambridge. He began his career as a journalist on the *Manchester Guardian* and the *Observer*. *Democracy* is the fourteenth of his plays, which include *Noises Off*, *Copenhagen* and *Wild Honey* (adapted from Chekhov's untitled play). Frayn has done a number of translations, mostly from the Russian. His novels include *Towards the End of the Morning* (in the USA, *Against Entropy*), *The Trick of It*, *A Landing on the Sun*, *Headlong* and *Spies*. Methuen has published two selections of his columns, *The Original Michael Frayn* and *The Additional Michael Frayn*. He is married to the biographer and critic Claire Tomalin.

by the same author

Novels

Headlong
A Landing on the Sun
Now You Know
The Russian Interpreter
Spies
Sweet Dreams
The Tin Men
Towards the End of the Morning
The Trick of It
A Very Private Life

Plays

Alphabetical Order
Balmoral
Benefactors
Clockwise (*screenplay*)
Clouds
Donkeys' Years
First and Last (*screenplay*)
Here
Jamie on a Flying Visit & Birthday
Look Look
Make and Break
Noises Off
Now You Know
The Two of Us
Wild Honey

Non-fiction

Constructions
The Additional Michael Frayn
The Original Michael Frayn
Speak After the Beep

Translations

The Cherry Orchard
Exchange
Fruits of Enlightenment
Number One
The Seagull
The Sneeze
Three Sisters
Uncle Vanya
Wild Honey

Democracy

Michael Frayn

Methuen Drama

Published by Methuen 2003

3 5 7 9 10 8 6 4

First published in 2003 by
Methuen Publishing Limited
215 Vauxhall Bridge Road,
London SW1V 1EJ

Methuen Publishing Limited Reg. No. 3543167

A CIP catalogue record for this book is available from the British Library.

ISBN 0 413 77382 5

Typeset by SX Composing DTP, Rayleigh, Essex
Printed and bound in Great Britain by
Cox & Wyman Ltd, Reading, Berkshire

Democracy

Democracy first premiered at The Royal National Theatre, London on 9 September 2003 with the following cast:

Günter Guillaume	Conleth Hill
Arno Kretschmann	Steven Pacey
Willy Brandt	Roger Allam
Horst Ehmke	Jonathan Coy
Reinhard Wilke	Paul Gregory
Ulrich Bauhaus	Paul Broughton
Herbert Wehner	David Ryall
Helmut Schmidt	Glyn Grain
Hans-Dietrich Genscher	Nicholas Blane
Günther Nollau	Christopher Ettridge

Director Michael Blakemore
Set Designer Peter J Davison
Costume Designer Sue Wilmington
Lighting Designer Mark Henderson
Sound Designer Neil Alexander

Characters (in order of speaking)

Günter Guillaume
Arno Kretschmann
Willy Brandt
Horst Ehmke
Reinhard Wilke
Ulrich Bauhaus
Herbert Wehner
Helmut Schmidt
Hans-Dietrich Genscher
Günther Nollau

Setting

A complex of levels and spaces; of desks and chairs; of files and papers; also of characters, who mostly remain around the periphery of the action when not actually involved in it, listening or unobtrusively involved in their work.

Act One

Darkness. The expectant murmur of an audience, silenced by a handbell.

Voice   Ladies and gentlemen, I declare the result of the vote to be as follows. Those in favour: 251. Those against: 235.

Applause, excitement. Lights up on **Brandt**.

I therefore declare . . . I therefore declare, according to article 63 paragraph 2 of the Basic Law, that the proposed Member has received the votes of the majority of Members of the Bundestag. Herr Brandt, do you accept election as Chancellor of the Federal Republic of Germany?

Guillaume (*with* **Brandt** *and* **Kretschmann**)   And for a moment time seemed to hold its breath. The world was about to change in front of our eyes. A Chancellor from the left again, after nearly forty years!

Kretschmann   Twelve years of Hitler. Four years of military government. Twenty years of conservatism and Cold War. And now a hope at last of ending the long stalemate in Europe.

Guillaume   Eleven twenty-two a.m., on the twenty-first of October, 1969 . . .

Brandt   Yes, Herr President. I accept the election.

Guillaume   Congratulations, tears. Willy Brandt had finally done it!

Kretschmann   And you were there in the Bundestag to see it.

Guillaume   An ordinary party worker from a humble district office in Frankfurt, up in Bonn for the day with a spectator's ticket. I shed a tear myself, I have to confess.

Brandt   I am grateful for the confidence that has been reposed in me. I am also a little proud. Almost forty years have passed since any member of the Social Democratic Party of Germany has held this office. Years during which this great party of ours, founded by a poor turner in Leipzig exactly a century ago to bring strength and hope to the oppressed, was brutally crushed by the Nazi state; years during which so many of our members underwent unspeakable sufferings in prisons and concentration camps, and so many of them met a violent death; years during which, after the end of the horror, we played our part, in city after city, in the resurrection of our nation from degradation and destruction, and in the miracle of its rebirth as a stable and decent society. No one can ever belittle what has been achieved in this country by people in all parties and of all persuasions. But on this day the war that Hitler waged, against the peoples of Europe and against so many of our own people, has finally been lost. We have a chance at last to create the Germany glimpsed by that ordinary Leipzig working-man a hundred years ago – a fatherland of love and justice.

Kretschmann (*with* **Guillaume**)   The most extraordinary thing of all, though, is what's happened to *you*. No one back home can believe it.

Guillaume   I can't quite believe it myself.

Kretschmann   You never seriously expected to see Willy Brandt elected Chancellor. Not in your wildest dreams, though, can you have imagined that three weeks later they'd be sending for you to join him.

Ehmke (*with* **Guillaume**)   Ehmke. Horst Ehmke. Willy's chief of staff. Running the Chancellor's office for him. Getting the whole enterprise up and running . . . (*With* **Wilke** *and* **Bauhaus**.) Thank you, Uli. Very helpful. Over there, if you would, on the desk . . .

Wilke   Not over there, if you please, Herr Bauhaus! Not on the desk!

Ehmke (*with* **Guillaume**)   Good of you to come in at such short notice. Listen, we need some fresh blood in here. And not just academics like me who learnt their politics at university. – Over here, Uli! Don't take any notice of Reinhard. – What we need is some of the lads from the party. People who can talk to people. Our colleagues in Frankfurt say you're just the type for us. Done wonders down there. Work all the hours God made. And I'm told you have a lively appreciation of our young friends on the left. All the idealistic young folk who've just put us into power. I believe you would describe them as . . .

Guillaume   Well . . .

Ehmke   Arseholes?

Guillaume   Arseholes.

Ehmke   Right – job for you. – The key to the drinks cupboard, Uli. I'm going to put it in your safe hands. – Chancellor's office. Liaison with the trade unions. Start Jan. 1. Yes?

Guillaume   Chancellor's office? Work there? You mean . . . with Willy?

Ehmke   Department III. Economic, Financial, and Social Policy. Federal salary scale IIa. Accept?

Guillaume   Yes, Herr Ehmke. I accept the appointment.

Kretschmann (*with* **Guillaume**)   So, you and Willy! Under the same roof! Starting your new jobs together!

Guillaume   I joined the party the year Willy became Governing Mayor of Berlin. Our stars are linked!

Kretschmann   You can't help laughing, though. Willy Brandt talks about the achievements of West Germany. Twenty years it's taken West Germany just to get its first mildly leftish government. Not a word about us over there in East Germany. No mention of what *we've* done in those same twenty years. We've actually built the socialist society they used to dream about!

Guillaume   Including the best foreign intelligence service the world has ever seen.

Kretschmann   Mischa Wolf asked me to give you his personal congratulations. This is the biggest feather in his cap yet. Our own man in the Federal Chancellor's office!

Guillaume   As long as Mischa's happy. That's all I want . . . And now here I am at work. A little room all to myself, up in the attics of the Palais Schaumburg. My first morning!

Ehmke (*with* **Guillaume**)   Would you step into my office for a moment, Herr Guillaume? One or two things we need to talk about.

Guillaume   – Personal welcome from the boss, even. Very charming.

Ehmke   Security want some questions answered. You left East Germany thirteen years ago. They've gone very carefully through your career in the West.

Guillaume   – Not a speech of welcome. A security vetting.

Ehmke   Freelance photography . . . photocopy shop . . . party work – it all seems to check out. Lot of unanswered questions, though, about what you were doing in East Berlin before you left.

Guillaume   – I wondered when it was coming. But out of the blue like that! Fright of my life. Somebody's obviously been telling tales. Two solid hours it goes on! Where? When? Who? In the end I have to lose my temper. – Herr Ehmke, escaping from East Germany means that you have to abandon everything you ever had in life. Your home, your friends, your family. For ever. And then you have to start life again from nothing, as nobody. You haven't had to do that, if I may say so. You can't begin to understand what it means. But now comes the bitterest part of all. You find

you're going to spend the rest of your life in your new
homeland under a black cloud of distrust and suspicion.
Thirteen years I've been here! The last nine of them
working night and day for this party! – Etcetera, etcetera. I
could hear the choke in my voice. And in the end . . .

Ehmke   Sorry. Have to put you through the hoops,
though. I have actually been doing a bit of checking with
your old boss in Frankfurt. Says he'd put his hand in the fire
for you. So what are we wasting each other's time for,
Günter? Let's get cracking!

Kretschmann (*with* **Guillaume**)   Your initiation rite.

Guillaume   And now of course he's my friend for life.

Kretschmann   So there you are, in the Palais
Schaumburg! What's it *like*? I'm blind, I'm deaf. You're my
eyes, you're my ears. I've got to paint the picture for
Mischa! You've got to paint it for me.

Guillaume   Towers, casements. A nineteenth-century
ironmaster's dream of the aristocratic life. Ghosts, of course.
From the Kaiser's time, from the Nazis. From the
Occupation. From Adenauer. And every now and then in
my office I hear a tiny ticking in the roof timbers.

Kretschmann   Deathwatch beetle. Symbolic, perhaps.

Guillaume   And every now and then Willy hears faint
sounds over *his* head. Footsteps. The scrape of a chair.

Kretschmann   That's you?

Guillaume   My office is directly above his.

Kretschmann   His own weevil in the woodwork. Can
you hear him?

Guillaume   Not a sound.

Kretschmann   Ear to the floor?

Guillaume   Nothing. He works very quietly. And when I
come downstairs . . .

Wilke (*with* **Guillaume**)   Herr Guillaume.

Guillaume   Günter! Please! Call me Günter!

Wilke   Settled in up there, are you, Herr Guillaume?

Guillaume   Snug as a bug, thank you, Reinhard. – Dr Reinhard Wilke. My immediate superior. The dragon guarding Willy's door. – Anything I can do for you, Reinhard? Filing? Copying? Watering the plants?

Wilke   Thank you, Herr Guillaume. We do have secretaries.

Guillaume   Extra pair of hands always available if you need them. No job too big or too small.

Wilke   I'm sure you have plenty to do upstairs.

Guillaume   – He's a little resistant to my charms. I'm not a prof or a doctor of anything, like all the others. – Just popping down to Party Headquarters. Anything you want me to take? Files? Papers?

Wilke   We have messengers, Herr Guillaume.

Guillaume   – I'll wear him down in the end.

Kretschmann   – Take your time. Don't rush it. We've waited thirteen years. We can wait a few more weeks.

Wilke (*with* **Ehmke**)   This Herr Guillaume of yours.

Ehmke   Good man. Just the type we need.

Wilke   Everyone in the office finds him a most surprising appointment.

Ehmke   Reinhard, we need to broaden our horizons in here. You're a lawyer, I'm a professor. We've all got dust in our hearts!

Wilke   But this wretched man has no professional training or experience of any sort whatsoever!

Ehmke   He's a trained photographer.

Wilke   So if we should need a souvenir of the staff outing . . .

Ehmke   He's also got practical experience of management.

Wilke   Management? Of what?

Ehmke   Of a photocopying shop.

Wilke   Horst, can we be serious for a moment?

Ehmke   Times have changed, Reinhard. We have to embrace the whole of society. Photographers. Managers of copy-shops. Women! We have to find some women, Reinhard, and embrace *them*!

Wilke   There's no shortage of secretarial staff. And as I understand it, Horst, they have been embraced by every government since the foundation of the Federal Republic.

Guillaume   – And now – the big day!

Kretschmann   – You met Willy?

Guillaume   – I'd just come downstairs and put my helpful smiling face round the door . . . – Would you like me to slip out for a sandwich, Reinhard? Oh, hello, Horst. How are things on your side of the corridor? Sandwich for you?

Wilke   Herr Guillaume, we must come to some understanding about access to this office . . .

Guillaume   – And suddenly, before he could push me out again . . .

Brandt   Capitalism stands on the brink of the abyss!

Wilke   Herr Chancellor . . .

Ehmke   Willy . . .

Brandt   And what's it doing there? Looking down on the Communists. And this is . . . ?

Ehmke   Herr Guillaume. Our contact with the unions.

Brandt   Oh yes. The owner of the footsteps.

Guillaume   – He knew who I was!

Kretschmann   – He knows who everyone is. Politician's trick.

Brandt   Another member of the Berlin Mafia, I believe. We Berliners have to stick together. They don't like us here in Bonn, Herr Guillaume.

Guillaume   No. When the Wall went up in sixty-one no one in Bonn lifted a finger. The only one who fought for us was you. We're never going to forget that. Particularly those of us who come from the other side. Those of us who know what it's like over there. – Sorry. Live with the wolves – howl with the wolves.

Brandt   East Berliner goes to the Stasi. 'My parrot's escaped.' Stasi: 'We don't do Lost and Found – we're the political police.' 'Exactly. I want it put on record that I don't share the parrot's political views.'

Guillaume   – He loves jokes. Particularly East German ones. – Why do the Stasi go round in threes? One who can read, one who can write . . .

Brandt   . . . And one to keep an eye on the two intellectuals.

Kretschmann   – You'll need fresher ones than that.

Guillaume   – I'm out of touch! Rush me the latest!

Brandt   My speech. Has it been typed?

Wilke   I'll send a messenger across.

Guillaume   *I'll* go! – And here I am! Fetching Willy's speech for him!

Brandt   Guillaume?

Ehmke   Günter Guillaume.

Guillaume   – I think I've caught his eye!

Brandt   He looks like the manager of a pornographic bookshop.

Wilke   He was in fact the manager of a photocopying shop.

Guillaume   Herr Chancellor . . .

Brandt   Thank you. Run off a few copies, will you, Reinhard?

Guillaume   I'll do it, Herr Chancellor.

Brandt   Oh yes. Your speciality.

Guillaume   Virtuoso of the Xerox machine. Confidentiality assured.

Kretschmann   – So we've got our foot in the door. Well done. Mischa's very pleased.

Brandt   I don't think I shall be able to stand very much of Herr Guillaume's company.

Ehmke   Willy, it's not good for you to be surrounded by professors and politicians. You need to keep some contact with the grass roots. You need some ordinary human being around who can tell you what people are thinking.

Brandt   Herr Guillaume, however, carries ordinariness a little too far. Find me someone else, will you, Horst?

Kretschmann (*with* **Guillaume**)   Now, here's how we're going to work. We're living in a goldfish bowl in Bonn – and if one of the goldfish keeps vanishing from sight people are going to notice. So we'll carry on meeting like this, quite openly, in the restaurants and bars where everyone goes. Two old friends having a drink together, where everyone can see us. Nothing passing between us. All photographs or photocopies of documents you'll hand over to your wife. She'll be your courier.

Guillaume   Poor Christel. She was the star of the show, not me!

Kretschmann   She did very well.

Guillaume   A job in the Hesse State Chancellery in Wiesbaden! What more could anyone hope for?

Kretschmann   One in the Federal Chancellery in Bonn.

Guillaume   Pure blind chance, Arno! A gift from the gods!

Kretschmann   Even the gods are working for Mischa.

Guillaume   It was her life, you know.

Kretschmann   Nevertheless, all written material to Christel. What Mischa really wants from you, though, is all the things that politicians and civil servants *don't* write down. The gossip. The background. The smell of things. The way they think. Who's in, who's out. Who's got their knife into whom. Copier and camera, certainly. But, above all, eyes and ears.

Guillaume   Willy keeps saying he wants to open their working procedures to public scrutiny.

Kretschmann   Here's how we can help him. And of course what we want to know about most of all is . . .

Guillaume   The Eastern Policy.

Kretschmann   The Eastern Policy. Any scrap of information that helps us judge his intentions towards the socialist block. Reconciliation, he says. Peace. But can we trust him? Is he really going to risk everything on such a gamble? 'Small steps', he says. How small? As small as the space he gives it in his speeches, slipped in below security and a lot of pious platitudes about 'daring more democracy'?

Brandt   – It was the historical achievement of my predecessors in this office to establish an understanding between Germany and its former enemies in the West. This understanding remains the basis of our political life and the guarantee of our security. But the division of the world into two great power blocs has torn Europe apart. It has split our country and our capital, and undermined our relationship with the peoples to the East of us. Our reconciliation with them is, as we all know, especially difficult. And yet it is as essential for peace as our reconciliation with the West.

Kretschmann   But will he really pay the price, when he comes right down to it? Is he really going to persuade people here to take their head out of the sand at last and recognise that we exist? You and me? The other Germany? Will he pay the final bill for the war: a quarter of Germany's lands lost to Poland and Russia – another quarter, us seceded and free. Half the nation, gone for ever!

Brandt   – Those who have been separated from their families, those whose homeland has been taken, will never forget what they have lost, and we can only try to understand and respect their grief.

Kretschmann   Twelve million people who have taken refuge here will never forgive him. Can any democratic politician simply write off a fifth of the population? He chooses his words so carefully. What do they mean?

Brandt   – Even if it is true that two separate states exist in Germany they can never be foreign to each other. We are bound by our language and our history, by our glory and our woe. We have even now common tasks and common responsibilities: for the peace between ourselves and for peace in Europe. Our unity is gone, and there is no way back. Step by step we must seek to ease the pain of separation. We must draw a line under the evils of the past. This government, then, will venture to open direct negotiations with Moscow, with Warsaw, and with East Berlin . . .

Kretschmann   But can we really trust him?

Guillaume   You can't help trusting him. When you're there in the audience. You look up at him – and there he is looking straight back at you. You personally. Talking to you alone. One human being to another.

Brandt – Dear friends, we must be at one with our neighbours. With all our neighbours – in the East just as much as in the West, within the German lands just as much as without. We must at last be reconciled.

Kretschmann   And then when you remember him in his Berlin days. When you think of all his efforts to stop West Berlin being reunited with the East. When he trots out his ancient East German jokes . . . Has he really changed? Or has he simply noticed that the young people in West Germany are all suddenly turning against capitalism and militarism? That the world is going our way? What does he say in private? In the office. Talking to his own people.

Brandt (*with* **Ehmke**, **Wilke** *and* **Guillaume**)   Can we trust them, though, Horst? When you look at their record. When you think of their total cynicism. What would people here say if they knew how East Germany tries to balance its trade deficit with us?

Wilke   I believe we may be about to venture onto rather sensitive ground here. Herr Guillaume . . .

Guillaume   Going, going!

Ehmke   No, let's try it on him. Ordinary voter. Our man in the street. Günter, this is something our new friends over there in the East don't want you to know about, for some strange reason. They have to find something to export to us. What's their one successful industry? The manufacture of political prisoners. So that's what they sell us. They arrest as many as they need, and we buy them out. A thousand or so a year at 40,000 Deutschmarks a head. Oh, and they also charge us for letting people out to be reunited with their families. So what do you think, Günter? Can we trust these new friends of ours?

Guillaume   – Yes? No? What do I say? Which one of me's going to answer?

Kretschmann – I leave it to you, Günter.

Guillaume – Leave it to which of me?

Brandt A difficult decision, evidently.

Guillaume Half of me wants to say one thing. Half of me wants to say another.

Brandt The position of the electorate as a whole on almost everything.

Ehmke I told you, Willy! Our man in the street!

Guillaume (*with* **Kretschmann**) *Do* we sell them political prisoners, though? Do we charge for family reunions?

Kretschmann Never mind about traitors and dissidents. What's worrying us now is the effect Willy's having on the rest of our people.

Wilke (*with* **Ehmke**)   His visit to East Germany.

Brandt – The most moving day of my life.

Wilke It starts as soon as his special train crosses the border.

Kretschmann Suddenly there he is amongst us. The first West German leader ever to set foot on East German soil.

Wilke Suddenly there it is all around us. The other Germany. The Germany we've never recognised. The Germany that doesn't exist.

Kretschmann Our people have never seen anything like it before. A living, breathing West German leader!

Wilke It's never happened before! In every town and village along the line – people with their hands outstretched towards him, people waving tablecloths and bedsheets. Armed police everywhere with orders to stop any demonstrations, but there's nothing they can do.

Kretschmann   This is why we need to make up our minds about Willy so urgently. Because we can't hold the lid on all this much longer.

Wilke   He gets to Erfurt for the summit meeting and they break through the police lines outside his hotel.

Kretschmann   It's terrifying, Günter.

Wilke   'Willy! Willy!' they shout. 'Come to the window!'

Kretschmann   There's only one person who can control them.

Wilke   'Willy! Willy!' they chant. 'The window!' He comes to the window . . .

Kretschmann   He looks down on all those upturned faces.

Wilke   What can he say that won't pour petrol onto the flames?

Brandt *gestures*.

Wilke   Silence. One of the greatest speeches of his career. Not a word. Just that one little gesture. That one characteristic little gesture.

Ehmke   I've seen him make it in Cabinet.

Wilke   'Calm down, calm down.'

Ehmke   Willy the peacemaker.

Wilke   A silent speech to a non-existent nation – and each person in the crowd feels he's being spoken to like a human being. Spoken to personally. One small gesture.

Ehmke   'Easy now! Easy does it!'

Wilke   But everyone understands another meaning altogether.

Ehmke   'Patience, patience. The time will come.'

Kretschmann   We're taking a huge risk here. Every word and gesture of Willy's raises the stakes. Every word and gesture of ours raises them again. He's going to sign treaties with Moscow, with Warsaw, with us. But can he get them through the Bundestag?

Guillaume   Majority of twelve.

Kretschmann   Twelve, yes. But only if the coalition holds together. It's all very well for Willy to cobble a government together by making a coalition with the Liberals, but how does he keep them in it?

Wehner (*with* **Brandt**, **Ehmke** *and* **Guillaume**)   Only thirty of them in the House to start with – and half of them don't want the Eastern treaties at any price.

Kretschmann   – This is the man who's got to make the coalition work?

Guillaume   – Herbert Wehner. Willy's party leader in the Bundestag.

Wehner   Three of them definitely going over. According to my private information. Three of them who find even desertion to the Christian Democrats preferable to the Eastern treaties.

Kretschmann   – Three of them going? Only take another three and the treaties are dead in the water. The whole Eastern Policy will have vanished like the morning mist.

Wehner   My sources tell me there's three more tender souls examining their consciences. Or the size of the offers they've had.

Kretschmann   – You're there? In the room with them?

Guillaume   – They've stopped noticing me.

Kretschmann   – So what does Willy say?

Guillaume   – Nothing. He won't look at Uncle Herbert. Uncle Herbert won't look at him. Long silences while Uncle sucks his pipe and rolls his thick wet lower lip.

Kretschmann   – 'Uncle Herbert.' They call Wehner that to his face?

Guillaume   – They don't dare. One look at that face and you can't say anything. It's like eating a persimmon. Your mouth dries. He appears on television and all the cats in Germany run under the sofa.

Wehner   Any fool could have seen this coming. We had a good stable coalition with the Christian Democrats.

Ehmke   As junior partners! Tied to a party that totally rejects any accommodation with the East!

Wehner   We were learning to govern. We're still learning. The party's not ready for office yet. But we pick up a few more votes, and what happens? Without consulting anyone our great captain cuts the tow and lashes us to the Liberals instead. To a leaking old tub of a party that's sinking in front of our eyes. We all knew this government wouldn't last for six months. So then what happens? Fresh elections? The Liberals drop one more point at the polls and they're out of the Bundestag altogether. Then we haven't got a coalition at all.

Guillaume   – You're getting all this? The man who's responsible for keeping the coalition going – and he's against it.

Ehmke   Herbert treats the party like a china teacup that's too precious ever to drink tea out of.

Wehner   Coalitions come and go. Parties remain. A coalition has no roots and no loyalties. A party has members and funds, offices and officers, patronage and punishments. We know we can rely on the loyalty of Herr Guillaume here because we know he's devoted his life to the party – and we know he's going to go on devoting his life to it because his job depends on it. And if any of our lads down there in the parliamentary party begin examining their consciences I'll begin examining their records.

Guillaume   – He's got files on all of them.

Wehner   I'll get Karl after them. They usually see sense.

Kretschmann   – Karl Tromsdorf?

Guillaume   – His private security service.

Kretschmann   – A highly reliable one. Learnt his trade with us. Old double agent.

Wehner   We've told the world we're going to 'dare more democracy.' Whatever that means. Let me tell you what I've learnt from bitter experience about democracy. The more of it you dare, the tighter the grip you have to keep on it. Not something that Number One wants to know about. He likes to look down at the end of a hard day's work and see two clean hands folded on the desk in front of him. But if the plumbing needs fixing someone's got to put their hands down the toilet. Never for one moment do I forget what finished representative government in this country in the thirties. Unstable coalitions, collapsing one after another like soap bubbles. It could happen again. Parliamentary democracy in Germany is still in its infancy. Without two strong legs to stand on it will go down to its enemies. One of those legs, whether we like it or not, is the Christian Democratic Party. The other one is this party of ours. Slowly, slowly, in these last twenty years, we've persuaded the electors to trust us. And now we've put our future into the hands of a dwindling band of dilettantes over whom we have no control at all. The Liberals. The name alone makes my blood run cold.

Kretschmann   – Old Communist himself, of course, Wehner. What would Willy's party do without us?

Brandt (*with* **Ehmke**)   He's never forgiven me for becoming Chancellor. Too spiritually disfigured to show his

own face, because every cat in Germany would be up the
curtains, and hates anyone who isn't. The puppetmaster
who's jealous of his own puppets. He wanted to keep a
Christian Democrat in the Palais Schaumburg just to keep
me out of it. An old Nazi! But then he knew how to pull his
strings. What a pair. The old Communist pulling the strings.
The old Nazi dancing on the end of them.

Ehmke   Discipline, Willy. That's what Uncle craves.
Someone to take the stick to him. That's what maddens him
about you, Willy. You won't take the stick to him. And
whatever you think about him, he's given his heart and soul
to this party.

Brandt   He gave his heart and soul to the Communist
Party. He also gave all his comrades away to the Russian
secret police.

Ehmke   He's still tormented by it.

Brandt   He's still as thick as thieves with his old mates in
East Berlin.

Ehmke   They've never forgiven him. They hate him.

Brandt   They understand each other, though.

Guillaume   – Do they?

Kretschmann   – Of course.

Ehmke   Anyway, he's a sentimental old thing, underneath
it all. The night you were elected he threw his arms round
you.

Brandt   With all the grace of someone's maiden aunt
making a drunken lunge at the postman.

Ehmke   He travels all over Germany visiting sick and
dying party members.

Brandt   Sits on their beds praying over them. First he's a
Communist, now he's a religious maniac.

Ehmke   Just as well there's no one can hear what you're like when you're like this.

Brandt   Only Herr Guillaume.

Ehmke   Oh – still here, Günter?

Brandt   How does Uncle know so precisely when people are dying, Herr Guillaume? Because, even if you're not dying when he arrives, after half-an-hour of his company you are.

Ehmke   Come on, Willy. These things get back to him.

Brandt   It's the only legal form of euthanasia.

Kretschmann   – I think you were a little soft on Willy when you started this job. What did I tell you, though? Wehner's not the only one with another side to him.

Guillaume   – No. Then there's Helmut.

Schmidt (*with* **Wehner**)   I revere Willy. You know I do. I always have. He's my political idol. I'd put my hand in the fire for him.

Kretschmann   – Helmut Schmidt. The heir to Willy's throne.

Schmidt   But his attitude to you is frankly ridiculous. Our majority's fast approaching zero. He knows he can't keep the party together without you.

Wehner   He also knows we can't get re-elected without him.

Schmidt   We all need each other! It's we three who made this party electable! You and Willy and I. We dumped the Marxism. We fought and fought. The three of us together. The Three Musketeers of modern socialism! I was so proud to be one of them!

Kretschmann   – Crown Prince Helmut. Waiting in the wings.

Guillaume   – And waiting there for ever. He's only five
years younger than Willy. Unless Willy gets run over by a
tram he'll be too old to inherit. That's his tragedy. That's
what makes him so edgy. That and his thyroid. He can't eat.
He's living on ice-cream and Coca-cola.

Kretschmann   – Ice-cream, Coca-cola, and the hope of
a runaway tram.

Schmidt   Willy always seems to be closeted with Horst
Ehmke these days.

Wehner   Herr Ehmke has a talent that some of the rest of
us lack: he appreciates the great man's jokes.

Schmidt   Most of them are about you, of course. You've
heard the one about you and the Virgin Mary?

Wehner   Yes. Thank you.

Schmidt   Meanwhile I have to sit there in Cabinet each
week and watch Willy let everything we fought for slip
through his fingers. He won't exercise any control! Won't or
can't. He claims to be interested in defence, but he won't
give me any support in preserving the department's budget!
He sits there saying nothing while Karl Schiller lectures us
by the hour on economics. It's like being back in college. All
those long silences of Willy's! All those compromises, all that
indecision. Anything to avoid confrontation or conflict.
(*With* **Brandt**.) So, Willy, yes or no? This draft or that
draft? My proposal or Karl Schiller's proposal?

Brandt   Let's talk about it. See if we can't find a solution
that keeps everyone happy.

Schmidt   You *can't* keep everyone happy, Willy! Not if
you're running a government! We've got to come to a
decision!

Brandt   Thank you, Helmut. What do the rest of us
feel . . . ?

Wehner   (*with* **Schmidt**)   The great peacemaker.

Schmidt   And I honour him for it, like the rest of the world. If only he wouldn't do it in private as well. I'm not the most patient of men, I accept that. But to sit there in Cabinet and *know* that I have the answer to a problem – and then to watch Willy piddle it away – it's more than flesh and blood can bear!

Wehner   And then suddenly, out of nowhere, some great gesture. Rushes us all into a new coalition without a word to any of us. All very fine, this wonderful spontaneity of his. But spontaneity's like democracy – it needs to be kept firmly under control . . . Can we help you, Herr Guillaume?

Guillaume   Sorry. Just looking for something. Don't mind me.

Schmidt   No, hand in the fire for him, it goes without saying. Hand in the fire.

Kretschmann   – The old Communist and the old Wehrmacht officer. Both yearning for long-forgotten discipline.

Guillaume   – Funny sort of discipline they practise, though. All they do is niggle away behind Willy's back.

Wehner (*with* **Ehmke** *and* **Guillaume**)   The great man at home again last night, I gather, to all his fashionable friends. Camelot-on-the-Rhine, by all accounts.

Ehmke   You should have been there.

Wehner   Curious, isn't it. Scarcely have we got the grimy old cloth cap off this party's head and wrenched the oily spanner out of its hands than the big chief's got us all into white tie and tails, drinking champagne out of actresses' slippers. No wonder they all love him. All the champagne-growers, at any rate. All the firms that rent out evening dress.

Schmidt (*with* **Wilke** *and* **Guillaume**)   Berliners! Not one of them who knows the value of money! We give them three billion marks a year to keep the city going, so they chuck it around as if it came out of the taps. And now of course Willy's letting them take over the whole government. It's like some kind of infestation!

Wilke   Even got them in here. Union business, Herr Guillaume?

Guillaume   Party business.

Wilke   Oh, yes, you've been promoted.

Schmidt   Not that Willy's even a real Berliner. He was born in Lübeck! So of course he has to be more Berlinish than all the rest of them.

Ehmke (*with* **Brandt** *and* **Guillaume**)   The problem with Uncle is very simple. He doesn't like you and you don't like him. The problem with Helmut is more complex. He loves you – and you don't love him back. He's like a sixth-former with a crush on the teacher. So he has to keep proving to her how much cleverer than her he is.

Wehner (*with* **Schmidt** *and* **Guillaume**)   Horst Ehmke closeted away with Number One again.

Schmidt   He's rapidly becoming Willy's Lord High Chamberlain. We're all going to end up taking our orders from him.

Wehner   He's certainly stepped in *your* light.

Ehmke (*with* **Brandt** *and* **Guillaume**)   Willy, what you need to do with both of them is to make them feel secure and appreciated. And the way to do that, Willy, if I may put it plainly, is to give them both the most colossal boot up the backside.

Guillaume   – And then underneath it all, gnawing away like rats at the foundations of the whole enterprise – the new left.

Genscher (*with* **Brandt**, **Ehmke**, **Nollau** *and* **Guillaume**)   This is our Achilles heel. People look at the government and what do they see? A lot of long-haired

radicals from the universities. People didn't like them when
they were rampaging round the streets in '68, and they
don't like them now.

Guillaume – Genscher. Minister of the Interior. He's
the one who's got to control the demonstrations.

Genscher Every time people turn on the television – yet
more violence by the left. They've held up a bank. They've
murdered a judge.

Ehmke That's Baader-Meinhof! The Red Army
Fraction! Nothing to do with our lot! Our lot wouldn't put
their thumb on a bedbug!

Genscher The left's the left. As far as most people are
concerned.

Brandt It was the young radicals who put us in office.

Ehmke We shove the old left off the raft before it finally
sinks under their weight, and as soon as the new left see it's
afloat they all scramble aboard and sink it again.

Genscher Then the next item on the news is the
Chancellor in East Germany having some kind of love-in
with the Communists.

Ehmke The Communists? What have the Communists
got to do with the left?

Genscher The left's the left! In any case Herr Nollau tells
me that East Berlin is giving active support to the terrorists.

Nollau We believe that the East German Ministry of
State Security is offering them refuge and training facilities.
We have evidence that it has been providing passage to the
Fatah camps in Syria and South Yemen.

Guillaume – Günther Nollau. The head of West
German Security . . . *Do* we support the terrorists?

Kretschmann   – Another of our defectors, Herr Nollau. Inspired choice for the job. Wanted for murder when he did his bunk.

Nollau   Nor, I may say, have the present negotiations with East Germany led to any abatement in the Ministry's campaign of espionage against us. We believe that East Berlin currently has something like a thousand agents active here.

Kretschmann   – Keep very still, Günter!

Guillaume   – They've forgotten about me. I'm the hatstand in the corner.

Nollau   There are almost certainly several hundred agents operating in government offices as this very moment . . . I understood this to be a private meeting.

Ehmke   Herr Guillaume. Works upstairs. One of us. Hates the left.

Brandt   Anyway, we no doubt have similar arrangements over there. Why not? We all speak the same language. I see the whole of Germany, East and West, as one gigantic glass palace.

Genscher   We must take security issues rather more seriously, Herr Chancellor. One more spy scandal and it could be the finish of this government.

Kretschmann (*with* **Guillaume**)   It could, Günter, it could. Keep very, very still under all those hats and coat.

Guillaume   In fact what finishes this government may well be Genscher.

Kretschmann   Genscher?

Guillaume   Liberal.

Kretschmann   Perfectly tame one.

Guillaume   Some of the more reactionary members of the Liberal Party don't think so. They want to make him

party leader. The first thing he'd do would be to abandon
Willy and go into coalition with the Christian Democrats.

Wehner (*with* **Nollau** *and* **Guillaume**)   The Foreign
Ministry. That's what his pay-off would be. That's what he's
got his eye on, and he knows Willy's never going to let him
near it. Trips to Paris and New York. Interviewed every
time he steps off a plane. If he appears on television often
enough he thinks one or two of the more observant voters
might start to notice his existence.

Guillaume   – Wehner and Nollau.

Kretschmann   – Always been as thick as thieves. Both
from Dresden, of course.

Wehner   So, what's the word inside the Liberal Party? Is
Herr Genscher taking over or isn't he?

Nollau   I've no idea. I'm not a Liberal.

Wehner   He's your Minister.

Nollau   You want me to spy on my own Minister?

Wehner   What's wrong with that? Equality before the
law. Just as long as Willy doesn't know. Clean hands! And
don't forget, you're not just an official of the government –
you're also a member of the party. You have a duty to
uphold the party's interests. Anything you get hold of, on
Genscher or anyone else – let me know. We have to stick
together, you and I. Two simple Saxons trying to survive in
a world full of cocksure Bavarians and devious
Rhinelanders. Two babes in the wood from Dresden, with a
wolf from Berlin lurking behind every bush.

Nollau   I'm very grateful for everything you've done for
me . . .

Wehner   So keep me informed.

Nollau   I always do.

Wehner   First. Yes?

Kretschmann (*with* **Guillaume**)   West Germany,
Günter! The Federal Republic! Not just one so-called
democracy – eleven separate democracies tied up in a
federation like ferrets in a bag! Eleven separate talking-shops
all talking at the same time, with the Federal talking-shop in
Bonn trying to make itself heard above the rest of them!
Three political parties, in and out of bed with each other
like drunken intellectuals, fifteen warring Cabinet Ministers
in Bonn alone, and sixty million separate egos. All making
deals with each other and breaking them. All looking round
at every moment to see the expression on everyone else's
face. All trying to guess which way everyone else will jump.
All out for themselves, and all totally dependent on everyone else. Not one Germany. Sixty million separate
Germanies. The tower of Babel! With not just one weevil in
the rafters, but weevils in every timber in the house. We have
our defects in the East, God knows we do. But at least we all
speak with one single voice. We all sing the one same song.
This is our strength. This is why we shall endure when this
whole ramshackle structure finally comes tumbling down.

Nollau (*with* **Wehner**)   One thing that might interest
you . . .

Guillaume   – Nollau to see Wehner this time. Something
about Genscher?

Kretschmann   – Leave it, Günter! Not twice running!

Guillaume   – Hatstand. No one notices it.

Kretschmann   – Hatstand keeps walking into the room
and they will.

Nollau   The security services are looking for a sleeper.
Someone inside our own party. I thought you might wish to
institute a few discreet inquiries of your own.

Wehner   A sleeper? What do we know about him?

Nollau   Not much. Planted at least a dozen years ago.
That was when we intercepted a radio transmission to him.

Ended with a personal message. Birthday greetings and congratulations on the arrival of his second son.

Wehner   Two sons? That's all we know?

Nollau   Also his name begins with G.

Guillaume   – Don't worry, Arno! The sky's clear!

Kretschmann   – A clear sky – that's just what the thunderbolt falls out of.

Ehmke (*with* **Guillaume**)   Could I have a private word, please, Günter?

Kretschmann   – I knew it!

Guillaume   – Hold on. Keep calm.

Ehmke   Party Conference next week in Saarbrücken. I'm setting up a temporary office for the Chancellor. You'll be running it. All right?

Guillaume   Of course. Anything. Always happy.

Ehmke   Going to be short-staffed, I'm afraid – you'll have to look after liaison with the security services. Sorry about that.

Guillaume   No – I've always had a secret interest in security. – You see? Just tossing another hat on the poor old hatstand.

Kretschmann   – Unbelievable. Only it's making me even more nervous.

Ehmke   Consolation prize, though, Günter. Egon Bahr's going to be negotiating in Moscow. You can have the use of his official car and chauffeur.

Kretschmann (*with* **Guillaume**)   Something's going to go wrong somewhere.

Guillaume   Don't worry! Willy's got the first treaty signed.

Kretschmann   Still Poland to go before he gets to us.

Guillaume   The Soviet one was the hard one. And it's the one that unlocks the door to all the others.

Kretschmann   It's not ratified yet. His majority's down to four. And if we lost Willy for any reason. A tram . . . a bus . . . a thunderbolt . . . A scandal of some sort . . . His private life, for instance. All these women he has . . .

Guillaume   Secretaries, journalists. Nothing serious these days. I've given you the list.

Kretschmann   If it got out, though . . .

Guillaume   Everyone knows!

Kretschmann   But doesn't say.

Guillaume   *We're* not going to mention it. Are we?

Kretschmann   Not us. We're trying to keep him on his feet. If ever Willy *did* lose his shine, though, Wehner would have him out like a bad tooth. Half a chance, that's all he and Helmut need . . .

Brandt (*with* **Schmidt**, **Wilke**, **Ehmke**, **Guillaume** *and* **Bauhaus**)   Uli!

Bauhaus   Chief?

Brandt   Bottles, glasses!

Kretschmann   – Drinking. He hasn't started drinking again?

Guillaume   – Not spirits this time. Only wine. They all do. By the bucket. Just wine, though, always wine. And always red, for some reason.

Kretschmann   – The last traces of their socialism.

Guillaume   – End of the working day they all get together with glasses in their hands. Relax. Forget their differences. Even Helmut. Even Wehner. And for an hour

or two all our problems are behind us. A little circle of
upturned faces, and after all that listening Willy talks at last.

Brandt   1945. Every city in Germany reduced to rubble.
So what did we start rebuilding with? The rubble. It was all
we had. Lines of women patiently sorting the usable bricks
out one by one. Passing them from hand to hand, cleaning
them, storing them . . . Who knows what buildings those
bricks had been part of? The cellars of the local SS . . . the
factories where the slave labourers suffered and died . . .
They cleaned up the bricks as best they could, and out of
them we built the plain straightforward cities we all live in
today. It was the same with the people. Who were the
people we rebuilt our shattered society with? Some of them
were survivors of the camps and prisons. Some of them were
exiles. But most of them had been the ordinary citizens of
the Reich. They were our building materials. We had no
other. And with those people we built the plain
straightforward institutions of the society we're all part of.
Now what confronts us? Two Germanies, broken apart like
the old shattered masonry. This is the material out of which
we have to build the world we're going to be living in
tomorrow. This is the only material we possess – the two
Germanies as they actually are. Riddled with doubts and
suspicions on both sides. If the building we're creating is
going to stay up, we have to make sure that this fragile stuff
will bear the load we're placing upon it. We have somehow
to find ways for the doubtful and the fearful on both sides to
accept what we're doing.

Schmidt   Willy's dream. Life without conflict.

Brandt   Conflict resolved.

Schmidt   Irreconcilables reconciled.

Brandt   Even the irreconcilables inside our own party.

Ehmke   Now there's a really solemn thought.

Brandt   One more solemn thought to carry with you into
the night, gentlemen, as you go back to your pining wives

and children, if you can still remember where they live:
under capitalism man is oppressed by man – under
socialism it's the other way round . . . Clear the desk, will
you, Uli. Work to be done.

Guillaume (*to* **Bauhaus**)   I'll help you.

Schmidt   Yes, where *do* our wives and children live . . . ?

Brandt   East Berlin sends one of its functionaries to the
West to report back on the death of capitalism. He goes to
London, he goes to Paris, he goes to New York. Gets back
to East Berlin. 'It's a beautiful death,' he says.

Wilke   Didn't try Bonn, I notice . . .

Wilke *and* **Schmidt** *go.*

Wehner   I wonder if Number One has ever asked Herr
Bauhaus what he feels about being used as his butler and
bottlewasher.

Brandt   Uli?

Ehmke   He's your bodyguard, Willy.

Brandt   No one's going to shoot me at this time of night.

Bauhaus   If there's nothing else, Chief . . .

Brandt   Wife and children, Uli.

Bauhaus   I'll be waiting with the car. (*Goes.*)

Ehmke   Does he *have* a wife and children, Willy?

Wehner   He probably can't remember any more.

Ehmke   Or Günter. Does *he*? You don't know, do you,
Willy. You've never talked to him.

Brandt   I asked you to get rid of Herr Guillaume.

Ehmke   Talk to him, Willy. He's devoted to you. All those
upturned faces gazing at you adoringly from the hall – he's
one of them. Talk to him. Find out what they're thinking
down there.

Brandt   He always reminds me of another Berlin speciality: meatballs cooked in fat. Very leaden and very greasy.

Wehner (*to* **Guillaume**)   Wives and children, yes . . . Grabert. G. Grabert would fit the bill. Horst Grabert. He a family man? You know all about us, Herr Guillaume. Does Horst Grabert have any children?

Guillaume   A boy and a girl. Why?

Wehner   Idle curiosity. Like to keep abreast of my colleagues' personal lives. Gaus. How about Herr Gaus?

Guillaume   Günter Gaus? One daughter.

Wehner   One daughter? Less trouble, perhaps, than a couple of sons . . . (*Goes.*)

Ehmke (*to* **Brandt**)   Talk to him!

Kretschmann   – So, now you're alone with him.

Brandt   No wife to go home to, then, Herr Guillaume? No children?

Guillaume   I'll wait till you've finished, thank you, Herr Chancellor. Make sure the spoons are locked up for the night.

Brandt   Though I gather you still find time to make yourself agreeable to one or two of the secretaries.

Guillaume   Oh . . . Just trying to be friendly . . .

Brandt   The Frankfurt party?

Guillaume   Me? Yes, I was.

Brandt   Know this man? Standing for party office down there.

Guillaume   Communist.

Brandt   Thank you. Helpful to know . . .

Guillaume   A wife, yes. I have a wife. You asked.

Brandt   In the same line of business as yourself, I believe?

Guillaume   She's transferred from Wiesbaden. We've found a flat in Bonn at last . . . You know there's something we've got in common, Herr Chancellor? You have a son called Peter – I have a son called Pierre. Fourteen. Somewhat different political views, though. Great lefty, your Peter, I know. Every time you open the newspaper – there he is, out on the streets again with his chums, protesting against his Dad's government. You must feel very . . . very proud of him . . . Whereas my Pierre is a tremendous fan of yours. Plastered 'Vote Willy' stickers all over the house.

Brandt   In bed by now. You never see him.

Guillaume   On Sundays. I try to make it up to him then. Our Sunday morning ritual – we jump in the car and drive out to the airport to fetch the papers. Wander round the airport together. Chat. I don't know what about. Watch the planes taking off. Imagine we're on one of them. Lifting away through the clouds. Up into the sunlight. Where are we going? No idea. Somewhere warm. Somewhere where the skies are blue and life is simple.

Brandt   Midnight, and a rather different Herr Guillaume begins to emerge. Something of a romantic, this one.

Guillaume   You know there's something you and I have got in common, Herr Chancellor?

Brandt   So, every Sunday morning. You and Pierre.

Guillaume   That's what I live for. Sunday mornings. Fetching the papers with Pierre.

Kretschmann   – You're not falling for him, like all the others?

Guillaume   – He listens! That's his trick. He listens to what other people say. Anyway, how can you see into someone's heart if you don't fall a little in love with them? And suddenly, out of nowhere, I hear my own voice speaking. – Herr Chancellor, you asked me once if you could trust them. The East Germans . . .

Brandt   You were in two minds, I recall.

Guillaume   – Midnight. No one but him and me, talking quietly together . . . – We have to trust each other, Herr Chancellor. There's no other way we can live.

Brandt   Thank you.

Guillaume   – Yes?

Kretschmann   – If you got away with it.

Guillaume   – I trusted him. And he trusts me. Then two days later . . . it's over.

Kretschmann   – Over? What's over?

Guillaume   – Everything! The whole project! The whole adventure!

Ehmke (*with* **Wilke** *and* **Guillaume**)   We're out! We're done for! There's no way we can win! Motion of no confidence, and five of our own people are going to rat!

Wilke   I believe Herr Wehner has turned one of them round again.

Ehmke   We're still going to lose. Out goes Willy. Out go all of us. In comes Barzel. In come the Christian Democrats.

Guillaume   Out go the Eastern treaties.

Ehmke   It's a squalid little procedural swindle. There are people out on the streets right the way across Germany.

Schmidt (*with* **Wehner** *and* **Guillaume**)   It was an accident waiting to happen. You set up a coalition like an egg balanced on the end of a billiard cue and sooner or later you have broken egg over the carpet. Not something that either of us would wish to remind Willy of now, but I have to say to you privately that this is precisely what you and I saw coming. I assume you've got one or two cards up your sleeve?

Wehner   Everyone waits for kind Uncle Herbert to do one of his party tricks. Even Number One. Just so long as I do it by magic. Just so long as he doesn't have to see the hidden springs and levers.

Guillaume   – Not for me to tell my masters what to do. But you said Mischa wanted me to use my political judgement, yes? My understanding of human psychology? I'll give it you in one word.

Schmidt   Money?

Guillaume   – Money.

Wehner   Is that what they call the stuff?

Guillaume   – Crisp crackling Deutschmarks.

Schmidt   You'd only need to pay two or three of that lot to abstain.

Guillaume   – Nearly two hundred and fifty of them to choose from.

Kretschmann   – Günter, you're becoming a little cynical.

Guillaume   – Why not, though? Mischa's done it before. What's wrong? We buy, we sell. Sell political prisoners – buy politicians. What's the difference?

Kretschmann   – Sixteen years of living in this place.

Guillaume   – *Do* we sell political prisoners?

Wehner   Clean hands. An interesting obsession for the man who claims to represent this country's manual workers.

Ehmke (*with* **Schmidt**, **Wehner**, **Wilke**, **Nollau**, **Genscher**, **Guillaume** *and* **Bauhaus**)   I've started shredding the files. I want every file of ours out of the office by the time Barzel moves in.

Wilke   He's already sent us the timetable. Fourteen hundred – result of the vote . . .

Schmidt   And it's late, it's late. What's the trouble? What's the hold-up?

Wilke   Fifteen hundred – he's appointed Chancellor; sixteen hundred – sworn in; seventeen hundred – moves into the Palais Schaumburg.

Ehmke (*to* **Guillaume**)   Here, Günter – grab. Dynamite. Handle them with your eyes shut.

Genscher   Here they come, here they come!

Nollau   We've lost.

Wehner   Wait.

Nollau   I happen to know.

Wehner   Wait, wait.

Nollau   I have my sources . . .

Schmidt   Look at Willy.

Genscher   On the scaffold.

Schmidt   As calm as a king . . .

Ehmke   Come on, come on . . .

Guillaume   They dragged people out of hospital!

Genscher   Poor old Guttenberg looks at the point of death.

Nollau   He is . . .

Ehmke   I don't think I can bear this . . .

Schmidt   Look, look! Sepp Woelker! He's signalling!

Wilke   Two! Two! He's signalling two!

Ehmke   They've done it!

Nollau   I told you.

Schmidt   By two votes!

Wehner   Wait . . . wait . . .

Schmidt   By two votes they've brought down the greatest leader this country ever had!

Wilke   Look at Willy.

Ehmke   He's *smiling* . . .

Guillaume (*with* **Kretschmann**)   And the whole party went mad! Not lost by two – *won* by two! Those bastards were so sure they'd got it in the bag! They had it all planned! Sworn in at four! Into the Palais Schaumburg by five! *We* thought they'd won! Got half the files shredded! Then out comes Sepp Woelker. Two, two, he signals. Oh *no* . . . !

Kretschmann   Well . . . congratulations.

Guillaume   Never mind football! Try parliamentary democracy! Sorry. Howling with the wolves.

Kretschmann   Howling with them? Or hunting with them?

Guillaume   Hunting with them, eating with them. Laughing with them, crying with them. No other way, if you're half man and half wolf.

Kretschmann   You won't forget the human half?

Guillaume   Don't worry. I shall remain the perfect servant of two masters. Mischa and Willy. Willy and Mischa. My two great masters. Tell me one thing, though. To satisfy my curiosity. How much did it cost?

Kretschmann   You're howling again, Günter.

Guillaume   Sorry. As long as Mischa's happy. That's all I want in life.

Kretschmann   And Willy.

Guillaume   And Willy.

Kretschmann   Back to work, then.

Wilke (*with* **Schmidt**, **Wehner** *and* **Guillaume**)   The Chancellor? Indisposed, I'm afraid, Herr Guillaume.

Schmidt   Another of his feverish colds.

Wehner   As they are known technically.

Schmidt   The doctor suspects that this one was brought on by the prospect of new elections.

Wehner   The doctor's with him now.

Wilke   Dr Ehmke.

Schmidt   Administering the usual medicine.

Wehner   Wielding the therapeutic corkscrew.

Schmidt   So do please take a seat. We're all waiting urgently for signs of recovery, and if past experience is anything to go by we may have to wait for some considerable time.

Guillaume   New elections?

Schmidt   Who knows?

Wehner   Ask Number One.

Schmidt   Join the queue.

Wilke   There *have* to be new elections. We've lost our majority in the House. We can't even pass the Budget.

Guillaume   We'll pick up votes.

Schmidt   The Liberals, however, will drop them. Will go below the five per cent mark. Will vanish altogether.

Wehner   And this misbegotten coalition with them.

Guillaume   So the Chancellor feels . . . ?

Schmidt   Ill, apparently, at the mere thought.

Wehner   Someone ought to take him another bottle of medicine.

Wilke   I suppose it should be me.

Schmidt   I think our little friend is already on his way.

Ehmke (*with* **Brandt** *and* **Guillaume**)   Come on, Willy. You're the Chancellor. Remember? So up you get and chancel.

Guillaume   Election candidate: 'If we win you'll get a new hospital – a new school – a new bridge over the river!' Voice from the crowd: 'We haven't got a river.' Candidate: 'You'll *get* a river . . . !'

Brandt   I can't face them, Horst. They look at me, and I see the perpetual question in their eyes. 'Why you? Why not me? Why *you*?'

Ehmke   They know the answer. Because you're the man you are.

Brandt   Whoever that is.

Ehmke   The man who's done all the things you've done.

Brandt   Done is done.

Ehmke   The man who's going to do all the things you're going to do.

Brandt   The man they hope I am, in spite of everything. The man they hope their hope will make me. The man they know they'll sooner or later find I'm not.

Ehmke   Up you get, Willy.

Brandt   All those expectant faces gazing up at me. I look down at them and I see always the same question, the same hope, the same dawning disappointment . . .

Kretschmann   – Shocked?

Guillaume   – Surprised. Never seen him in one of his depressions before.

Kretschmann   – Disillusioned?

Guillaume   – Disarmed.

Brandt   And when I think of the jibes that come out at every election. The sneers about my illegitimacy. The taunts about being a traitor. What was I doing during the war, eating smorgasbord in Scandinavia while all the rest of them were trapped inside the charnel-house? I came back with clean hands! That's what they cannot bear.

Ehmke   It's themselves they demean, Willy, not you.

Brandt   I think the time has come for me to step down.

Schmidt (*with* **Wilke**, **Wehner** *and* **Guillaume**) Resigning?

Guillaume   Talking about it.

Wehner   Of course.

Schmidt   Talking, though. Talking's a good sign.

Wehner   I have some sympathy with him, I have to admit. They skinned *me* alive for my exile.

Schmidt   You were a Communist. You got your hands dirty. You were part of the great train-wreck of German history like all the rest of us. Even our chirpy friend here from Berlin, no doubt. What, seventeen at the end of the war, Herr Guillaume?

Guillaume   Eighteen.

Schmidt   Hitler Youth? Boy soldier?

Guillaume   Of course. Anti-aircraft. Like you.

Wehner   All of us on the train, except the great man himself.

Schmidt   On the boat to Norway instead.

Wehner   He leaves here each night and he turns back into
a Norwegian. The German Chancellor – and he speaks
Norwegian with his wife and children.

Schmidt   He came back in 1945 wearing Norwegian
uniform.

Wehner   Those beloved Berliners of his scrabbling like
pigs in the dirt for scraps, and where was the great man?
Sitting at table with the Occupation forces, eating with
commandeered silverware off commandeered china. His
hands as clean as ever.

Schmidt   This is Willy's great strength. He's not quite one
of us. He doesn't quite understand what all the rest of us
understand.

Kretschmann (*with* **Guillaume**)   You look as if you
could do with a spoonful or two of the red medicine
yourself.

Guillaume   They've got Karl Schiller out of Economics
and Finance. Trapped him into resigning. Helmut's taken
them both over.

Kretschmann   One step closer to the throne.

Guillaume   Also things are a little bleak at home.

Kretschmann   Christel?

Guillaume   Silences. Tears.

Kretschmann   I'm so sorry.

Guillaume   She seems to have been doing a little spying
on her own account.

Kretschmann   This is the secretaries?

Guillaume   Etcetera.

Kretschmann   You've told her it's purely professional?

Guillaume Etcetera, etcetera. It's the profession that's finished us. She gets homesick, Arno. Don't you ever feel a sudden longing to be over there again?

Kretschmann Of course.

Guillaume It comes at the oddest moments.

Kretschmann Those quiet grey streets. That blessed dullness.

Guillaume That simplicity.

Kretschmann We smuggled you back a couple of times.

Guillaume Like a returning ghost. Sworn to silence and invisibility. Eavesdropping on my own absence.

Kretschmann So West Germany has not proved to be the paradise that so many of our fellow-citizens think it is.

Guillaume She wants a divorce, Arno.

Kretschmann She can't have one. Mischa won't let her. We need you as a couple. And think about Pierre.

Guillaume I think about him all the time.

Kretschmann Your Sunday mornings at the airport together.

Guillaume Even that's just the cover for a letter drop.

Kretschmann Every coin has two faces.

Guillaume If I'm arrested . . .

Kretschmann Why should you be?

Guillaume It can't go on, Arno! Not for ever! And when they arrest me they'll arrest Christel.

Kretschmann Pierre would be looked after. I promise you.

Guillaume He's only fifteen. He wouldn't understand.

Kretschmann It would all be explained to him.

Guillaume   I wake sometimes at night, and I feel a sick dread creeping through my body.

Kretschmann   You and Willy. You're like some old couple who've been married for forty years. He goes down so you go down. He comes up again and . . .

Ehmke (*with* **Guillaume**)   Günter! A little light bedtime reading!

Guillaume   The railway timetable?

Ehmke   Elections in November. Willy's going to be out campaigning in his special train.

Guillaume   The train? It's his personal assistant who organises the train. Peter Reuschenbach.

Ehmke   Standing for election. You'll have to take over.

Guillaume   As Willy's . . . personal assistant?

Ehmke   Bit of a killer, I'm afraid. Train, files, his dispatch-boxes, all incoming and outgoing correspondence – the whole works. Sorry, but *someone's* got to do it, and – there you are.

Kretschmann   – Pinch me, will you?

Guillaume (*with* **Brandt**)   – And now everything changes. For days at a time our home becomes this luxurious suite of softly rolling rooms. They're fitted out in rosewood and teak, in walnut and mahogany and cherry, and they once bore Reichsmarschall Göring around the Nazi empire. Now they're bringing Willy to ask the electors of Germany for their votes.

Brandt   Dear friends, I say to you and I say to all our people: have the courage to show compassion.

Guillaume   – Compassion. This is the party's election slogan. But on the hoardings everywhere he goes there's a simpler message: Willy!

Brandt   Compassion for those nearest to you!
Compassion, too, for those who are not so close!

Guillaume   – 'Willy must stay Chancellor! Willy! Willy!'
And always, in the shadows at Willy's side – Günter. The
master of the timetables – the high priest of the holy book.
The major-domo of our little travelling court. The personal
valet. The bearer of the official dispatch-case.

Brandt   Where's this?

Guillaume   Berneburg, Chief. – 'Chief', you notice. Not
'Herr Chancellor'. Not on the train. Picked it up from Uli.

Brandt   And we arrive Hildesheim . . . ?

Guillaume   1207. Seven minutes handshaking Town
Hall – ten minutes discussion Mayor – three minutes
Register Office spontaneous with bride and groom . . .

Brandt   This is where I feel at home, Herr Guillaume. On
the move. Fourteen years I spent in exile. Fourteen years of
travelling for the cause and eluding the Nazis. Norway,
Sweden. Spain, France. Then nearly twenty years going
back and forth between Berlin and Bonn. Going round and
round the world, telling everyone 'Berlin, Berlin'. Thirty or
forty years of my life looking out of trains and planes at
other lands and other lives.

Guillaume   Speech Town Hall . . . Unemployment
figures . . . Federal investment . . . Local anecdote . . .

Brandt   I get so much more done on the train. No Uncle
to suck his pipe at me. No Helmut to lecture me.

Guillaume   – No Wilke to keep me away from Willy. No
Ehmke to listen to his stories.

Brandt   No wife. No family.

Guillaume   – Just me. Getting his suit pressed. Laying it
out with the matching shirt and tie. Taking the telexes back
and forth to the wireless car.

Brandt   These two are urgent. This one's confidential.

Guillaume   I'll get it ciphered. Never know who's going
to see these things in transit. – Every communication he has
with the outside world – it passes through me. The knight
errant and his loyal squire. The travelling magician and the
assistant who knows all his tricks. Everything he sees – I see
it, too.

Brandt   All those other worlds! That little factory on the
industrial estate. I could be working in there . . . And
already it's gone . . . The bent old man in that village street,
turning to glance up at the passing train . . . That could
have been me instead of him . . . I could be in that silver
Mercedes on the autobahn, vanishing into another distance
altogether . . . We're stopping.

Guillaume   Nordstemmen. Three minutes. A few words
from the window. – And there they are, the good people of
Nordstemmen.

Brandt   Not a bad house.

Guillaume   – The same sort of dutiful supporters we've
seen waving and smiling in Northeim and Freden and
Alfeld.

Brandt   Dear friends! Have the courage to show
compassion . . . !

Guillaume   – Which of the women has he got his eye on
this time? Is it that one at the front gazing up at him with
very slightly parted lips? Or the one over there smiling that
strange dark half-smile? Or both of them at once? Or all of
them? Each one of them knows he's looking at her, and her
alone . . .

Brandt   I can see you, Herr Guillaume. Eyeing the girls.

Guillaume   What is it about women, Chief?

Brandt   The way they look at you . . . The way they look straight into your eyes and you look straight into theirs. The way you can't understand them. The way you can.

Guillaume   The way they smile.

Brandt   The way they look seriously at you. The way they make fun of you.

Guillaume   The way they're not like men.

Brandt   The way they are. The way they touch your hand. The way they touch your face. The softness of their touch on your skin. The softness of your own on theirs . . . All the different people you can be with them. All the different ways your life might go . . .

Guillaume   – But already they're slipping away from us. All those sweet possibilities – vanishing for ever . . . And when the evening comes . . .

Brandt   Uli! Where are you?

Bauhaus   Chief. (*Offers wine.*) Red or red?

Guillaume   – He relaxes and he talks, the way he does at the end of the working day in Bonn. But now there's no Uncle Herbert, no Crown Prince Helmut, no faithful Ehmke. Only the journalists travelling with us. Only Uli. And sometimes – only me. Nobody. An upturned face like all the others.

Brandt   I've been trying to remember a boy I used to know when I was growing up in Lübeck. Strange lad. Always rather solemn and serious. Not much fun in his life. Never quite enough to eat. No money. No friends. No father. Not much of a mother, for that matter. Brought up by his grandparents . . .

Guillaume   And this boy was called Herbert Frahm?

Brandt   Herbert Frahm. The name's as odd as everything else about him . . . Then one day, when he was nineteen years old, he vanished off the face of the earth. He set out

from Lübeck to go to Dresden, and he never arrived. Well,
this was 1933, and my celebrated predecessor with the little
moustache had just taken office. People had a habit of
vanishing then, in one way or another. Not a good time to
be a member of a left-wing party, as Herbert Frahm was.
Not a good time to be going to its annual conference. Only
one bit of Herbert Frahm ever arrived in Dresden. His old
student cap. But now it was perched on the head of a young
man no one had ever seen or heard of before.

Guillaume Willy Brandt.

Brandt That's the strangest thing of all about Herbert
Frahm. The fact that I was him, and he was me. What was
it like, being him? I look back, and all that time has
vanished behind a thick grey veil, like the old Lübeck
waterfront in the fog on a winter morning. What became of
him, when Willy Brandt took over his body and his student
cap? Sometimes I catch a glimpse of him. Out of the
window of the train. In a waiting crowd. A solemn boy,
glancing up at me with a speculative look in his eye. What
does he make of me? But then he turns, and goes away into
some other life where I can never follow . . . You had a
father, Herr Guillaume?

Guillaume Café pianist.

Brandt An honourable vocation.

Guillaume He was also a Nazi. And when he came back
at the end of the war and found my mother with another
man he jumped out of the window. It was a high window.

Brandt Two fatherless boys, wandering the world looking
for . . . what are we looking for?

Guillaume I don't know, Chief. Women?

Brandt Günter! I'm shocked!

Guillaume – 'Günter', though! 'Günter'!

Bauhaus Sorry, Chief . . .

Brandt   What is it, Uli?

Bauhaus   One of the journalists is getting a bit impatient. Says you promised to do an interview before we get to Kassel.

Brandt   Günter and I are talking. Tell him I'll do it tomorrow.

Bauhaus   Her.

Brandt   Her? Oh, yes. *Her*. Well . . . I suppose we have to keep the press happy.

Guillaume   I'll be just the other side of the wall, Chief, if you need me.

Brandt   I think I can manage a press briefing on my own, thank you, Günter. So she's . . . ?

Bauhaus   In your compartment. I've taken the files off the bed.

Brandt   And we arrive Kassel . . . ?

Guillaume   In forty-five minutes. Witzenhausen first, though.

Brandt   Word from the window?

Guillaume   And . . . jacket and tie, Chief!

Brandt   Trousers?

Guillaume   Certainly. (*With* **Bauhaus**.) Pretty, this one?

Bauhaus   I wouldn't know.

Guillaume   Eyes closed while you searched her?

Bauhaus   You find all this very amusing.

Guillaume   You did give her a full body-search?

Bauhaus   *I* find it pretty distasteful.

Guillaume   I sympathise. Terrible job.

Bauhaus I've got a wife and children.

Guillaume *He's* got a wife and children.

Bauhaus Oh, really?

Guillaume So for all we know she may be wired? May even be working for *them*?

Bauhaus Wouldn't put it past them.

Guillaume – *Not* one of ours, is she?

Kretschmann – Not my department, women. I'm pleased to say.

Guillaume Or Baader-Meinhof. Gun in her knickers. Put your ear to the wall, Uli!

Bauhaus Note the time in, note the time out. That's all I'm required to do.

Guillaume Just take the dispatch-case into my compartment for me, then. And, Uli . . . Any more young ladies who want a briefing – any hour of the day or night – my compartment is next door to the Chief's. – And on we go. Trip after trip. Week after week. Kiel, Karlsruhe . . . Bremen, Brunswick . . .

Brandt Dear friends. Have courage . . .

Guillaume – Everywhere, as the campaign goes on, the upturned faces become more radiant, the outstretched hands more clamorous to touch him. Willy passes among them like a Messiah. Smiling, smiling . . . Speaking, speaking . . .

Brandt The courage to show compassion . . .

Guillaume – And always, a few discreet paces behind him, his loyal servant, his faithful friend.

Brandt The courage to love your neighbour . . .

Guillaume – He asked Horst Ehmke to get rid of me. I found the memo. My personality was one of the things that depressed him, he said. I was hurt. Naturally. But I put it behind me. It was the depression speaking. I've forgotten all about it. So has Horst, by the look of it – because here we are, the Chief and I, together still, closer than ever.

Brandt   The courage to find your own true self . . .

Guillaume   – Willy and Günter. The noble hero and his comic servant. Don Quixote and his Sancho Panza. Over and over again he gazes down on those upturned faces. Over and over again he speaks, until his throat's raw.

Brandt   Dear friends . . . dear friends . . .

Guillaume   – Some of the older women weep, and press amulets and rosaries into his hands for him to bless. And as for the younger women . . .

Bauhaus (*with* **Guillaume**)   Look at them out there! It's worse than a rock concert! How am I supposed to cope with that mob? Soon as he shows his face they're going to rush him.

Guillaume   I'll help you, Uli. They won't get past us! Only one or two of the very prettiest ones, perhaps.

Bauhaus   Supposing they were *your* daughters.

Guillaume   We're public servants, Uli. We have to respect the voters' wishes.

Kretschmann   – Don Quixote and Sancho Panza? Or Don Juan and Leporello?

Guillaume   – You sound almost as sour as Uli.

Kretschmann   – The free society, Günter. Enjoy it while you may.

Guillaume (*with* **Brandt**)   – The softness of their skin. The light in their eyes. Or the warmth in their hearts. Something that got left behind in the mists of Lübeck all those years ago . . . No? No, very well. Just a thought. Forget it. He's a bit of a lad, that's all. We're two lads

together. Two fellows on the loose. Two travelling salesmen
away from their wives. But what a product we have to sell!
Willy Brandt, the saviour of Europe, the greatest statesman
in the world, with the Nobel Peace Prize to certify it. The
Moscow treaty – signed and ratified. The Warsaw treaty –
signed and ratified. Yes, and in Warsaw he achieved
immortality. He left a single image in the memory of the
world that no one will ever forget . . .

Ehmke   – Another of his unspoken speeches, and the
greatest of them all.

Guillaume   – He lays his official wreath at the
monument to the murdered Jews of the Warsaw Ghetto. He
steps back. And then . . .

Schmidt   – Something else. He's going to do something
else . . .

Guillaume   – For a moment once again time seems to
hold its breath. Once again the world is about to change in
front of our eyes. And out of nowhere . . .

Brandt *kneels*.

Guillaume   – For a moment I think, 'No, no, no! This
time he's gone too far!' But I'm wrong, and he's right,
because this is what the world remembers. That long
moment when the German who has no cause to kneel went
back down into the lowest depth of German history and
knelt for all of us. The one unspoken word that said
everything he longed to say. The one simple gesture that
embodied everything he was loved for and everything he
was loathed for.

Wehner   – Something speaks in him, and he hears it.

Schmidt   – Some small voice that speaks to him, and to
none of the rest of us.

Guillaume   – I wept, Arno.

Brandt *rises*.

Kretschmann – Perhaps at last the wounds are beginning to heal. Perhaps the irreconcilables are beginning to be reconciled.

Guillaume – Ten days before the election and they sign the treaty between the two Germanys. The keystone of the Eastern policy locked into place.

Kretschmann – Because you helped us to trust him.

Guillaume – And on election night, who is it who brings the good news to Willy? – (*with* **Brandt**, **Wehner**, **Schmidt**, **Ehmke**, **Genscher**, **Wilke**, **Nollau** *and* **Bauhaus**.) May I be the first to offer my congratulations, Chief? They're saying two hundred and seventy-one seats! They're saying a clear forty-six-seat majority!

Wehner Our best result ever!

Genscher Even the Liberals have picked up another eleven seats!

Wehner Right across the board! Swing voters in the middle. Catholic workers. Old ladies. The young.

Genscher Willy, we've had our differences, and we'll have more in future. But let's make no mistake about it. This is your victory.

Schmidt We planted the seed of this when we reformed this party ten years ago. You and Herbert and I. And now we harvest the golden fruit.

Wehner Here – a hug from your wicked Uncle.

Wilke Congratulations, Herr Chancellor. On behalf of everyone in the office.

Nollau And everyone in Federal security.

Bauhaus Also from your barman and bouncer.

Guillaume May I say, Chief, that working with you has been the best thing that ever happened to me, or ever will?

Ehmke Willy, your long exile is over at last.

All Speech! Speech!

Wilke He can't speak!

Ehmke He's spoken himself hoarse!

Schmidt Come on, Willy!

Ehmke Make the most of it, Willy! It's all downhill from now on!

Brandt Dear friends . . .

Ehmke He can still say *that*!

All Listen! Listen!

Brandt This is of course a victory for all of us here who have worked so hard together. But it is more than that. It is the German people's endorsement of the great reconciliation that we have begun. Never before, never before, has a German state lived in such harmony both with the free spirit of its citizens and with its neighbours.

Guillaume (*with* **Kretschmann**) And on into the night the celebration goes. Parliamentary democracy, Arno! One unending wild party! You're on your feet – you're on the floor! They've thrown you out – you've got back in! Now everyone's singing – now they're fighting. Now they're weeping – now they're laughing. Now someone's passed out behind the sofa – and it may be you.

Kretschmann Now someone certainly needs a strong black coffee.

Guillaume I'll be sober enough in the morning, never you fear. We'll all be sober.

Wehner (*with* **Schmidt**) So, what does the world look like in the cold grey light of day? I'll tell you what I see. Another four years of indecision. Another four years of compromise and drift. Another four years of Willy.

Schmidt   Another four years of sudden unscheduled gestures. There'll be no holding him now. He'll be more intoxicated with success than he ever was on red wine or schnapps.

Wehner   He needed his old friends before to control the party and hold the coalition together. Now he won't need us any more.

Ehmke (*with* **Schmidt** *and* **Wehner**)   Listen, jobs in the new government. Who gets what. The usual horse-trading. You two gentlemen are going to have to stand in for Willy and preside over the negotiations.

Wehner   Not another feverish cold?

Ehmke   His throat. The doctors won't allow him to speak. On his way into hospital for tests. Here – letter from him. This is how he wants you to do it.

Wehner (*with* **Schmidt**)   So, the game begins once more.

Schmidt   Only now ministers are handed their instructions by the Lord High Chamberlain.

Wehner   I shall put them carefully away in the inmost chamber of my briefcase.

Schmidt   Better look first. See who's in, who's out.

Kretschmann   – *You're* in, are you?

Guillaume   – I'm waiting for Ehmke to tell me.

Kretschmann   – He told Ehmke to get rid of you.

Schmidt   So, what does Willy say?

Wehner   Not much, I imagine, if he can't speak.

Schmidt   In the letter. The letter Ehmke gave you.

Wehner   Ehmke, yes . . . I know you've always felt he might benefit from a change of job himself.

Schmidt   Broaden his experience. Give him a new perspective.

Wehner   Which department do we feel would suit his talents best?

Schmidt   The Post Office needs reorganising. He might find that an interesting challenge.

Wehner   He knows a lot about carrying messages.

Schmidt   Does Willy say anything about him in the letter?

Wehner   What letter?

Schmidt   You put it in your briefcase.

Wehner   Oh, dear God, I've lost it. Can't find it for the life of me.

Schmidt   So . . . Ehmke gets the Post Office, then?

Kretschmann   – And what *does* Ehmke say?

Guillaume   – Nothing. No Ehmke. – Have *you* seen him? Horst Ehmke?

Wehner   Taking a little well-deserved holiday, perhaps. Oh, and Herr Guillaume. Your family. Are they well?

Guillaume   In rude health, thank you.

Wehner   Two sons, is it?

Guillaume   Just one.

Wehner   Of course. I'm glad to hear it.

Kretschmann   – No Ehmke? What does that mean?

Guillaume   – It means that Willy will have to look me in the eye and tell me himself. (*With* **Brandt**.) So what's been decided, Chief? Am I staying with you? – Not a word! He simply . . . hands me the dispatch-case. Another of his silent gestures! And what this one means is: 'Yes! On we go! To the bitter end! Together!'

Darkness.

Act Two

Guillaume (*with* **Brandt** *and* **Kretschmann**)   Nothing in this world turns out the way anyone expects. Nothing! I look at Willy sometimes and it breaks my heart. Everything he ever wanted he gets. The election. The treaties. Even the treaty with us that crowns the whole enterprise. And at once everything goes wrong. Everything! Inflation, rising prices, impossible wage demands, industrial chaos . . .

Kretschmann   Democracy, Günter! Sixty million separate selves, rolling about the ship like loose cargo in a storm.

Guillaume   They've hauled the monument into place. And now they've dropped the ropes there's nothing to keep them together. They're like tired children at the end of the holiday, with nothing left to do but squabble.

Schmidt (*with* **Wilke** *and* **Wehner**)   Will someone kindly tell me how the Cabinet can discuss the Foreign Ministry's proposals for arms reduction when the Foreign Ministry still hasn't tabled them?

Wilke   There seems to have been some slight confusion over the date . . .

Schmidt   No doubt on the part of the same nameless person who arranged for the Chancellor to give a press conference on tax-reform the day before we decided what the policy was.

Wehner   On the other hand we've launched a major new policy initiative. Or so I read in the press.

Wilke   A leak, I'm afraid.

Wehner   A pilgrimage to find the New Middle.

Schmidt   The New Middle? What happened to the old one? Which is where Herbert and I have been struggling to keep this party for the last ten years.

Wilke   I believe the idea originated with the Press Office.
As I understand it, the intention is to provide some sort of
counterpoise to the left.

Wehner   We shouldn't need a counterpoise if Number
One hadn't got them worked up by all his talk about daring
more democracy.

Schmidt   What is happening to this government? We
casually launch into wild schemes without any proper
consultation. We take on new commitments without any
idea how they're going to be funded. When Horst Ehmke
was running the Chancellor's office he used to co-ordinate
this kind of thing.

Wehner   The great man in his wisdom decided to
dispense with Horst Ehmke's services.

Schmidt   But Grabert's in charge here now! Why can't he
do it?

Wilke   Dr Grabert is away this week.

Guillaume   In Siberia.

Schmidt   *Siberia?*

Wilke   On his way to Tokyo.

Schmidt   A treaty with Japan?

Wilke   A study of airline development.

Guillaume   A freebie.

Schmidt   Another Berliner, of course.

Wehner   This government is falling apart in front of our
eyes.

Schmidt   Because Willy does nothing! Nothing, nothing,
nothing!

Guillaume (*with* **Brandt** *and* **Kretschmann**)   Nothing.
It's true. I wait in the shadows at his back on provincial
railway stations, willing him to speak, as if he were Pierre,

five years old still and standing dumbstruck in the school
nativity play. He gazes out over the expectant faces, and –
not a word. Not a gesture. Not a smile or a frown. His face
is a mask. A mask with no one behind it. The people gaze at
the effigy of their Chancellor. The effigy gazes back. His
famous silence. But this time what it says is – nothing.

Schmidt (*with* **Wehner**, **Wilke**, *and* **Guillaume**)   Where
is he now? Not another feverish cold?

Wehner   Or still brooding about his operation?

Schmidt   *Other* people have medical problems. They
manage not to let it affect their behaviour . . . What?

Guillaume   I didn't speak.

Schmidt   I'm perfectly prepared to subscribe to the
general belief that Willy is God. What I find a little
confusing, though, is not knowing which Person of the
Trinity he's going to be from one moment to the next – God
the Father or Christ crucified. Saving your presence,
Herbert.

Wehner   Our great leader's jibes have inured me to any
insult to my beliefs.

Schmidt   Most of them you never even heard when Horst
Ehmke was around to control things.

Ehmke (*with* **Brandt**)   We won. That was our great
mistake, Willy. Defeat is the only thing that this party
understands. Defeat is a testimony to high ideals. Defeat
makes no demands. Victory means you have to *do*
something – and *doing* something always involves dissent and
compromise and making mistakes.

Brandt   Even you seem to have abandoned me.

Ehmke   I'm reorganising the Post Office. The job you
gave me. You sacked me, if you remember, Willy.

Brandt   I saw a boy watching me the other day. In the
crowd on a station somewhere. Fifteen, sixteen. Very

solemn and unsmiling. Some kind of cap on his head, like an old-fashioned student's cap. I couldn't take my eyes off him. He just gazed back at me. Gazed and gazed, and never a smile. He didn't like what he saw.

Ehmke   Don't worry about the radicals.

Brandt   I watched him. He watched me. Until we vanished from each other's sight again.

Guillaume   Shall I send Uli out for a packet of cigarettes, Chief? – He's trying to give up smoking, on top of everything else.

Brandt   That operation, Horst . . .

Ehmke   Operations are like everything else, Willy. They sometimes go wrong.

Brandt   I thought I was going to die. I came round in the middle. I couldn't breathe . . . Solve everything, wouldn't it. Helmut would take over. Uncle would come back into the party leadership. Genscher would become Foreign Minister, and be kissed by the television lights and changed into a prince.

Guillaume   – He nearly died again in Israel, in that helicopter on top of Masada. A sudden gust of wind, and it slides away like a fallen leaf. Stops at the very edge of the drop. Uli shouts 'Everybody out!' And the Chief just sits there, not moving, looking down into the Dead Sea valley four hundred metres below.

Brandt   It's waiting so quietly and patiently, the earth down there. Smiling, arms outstretched, like a mother waiting for her child to run to her . . . I don't fear death. Only the agonising struggle to breathe until death comes, only the long fall . . . Only opening my eyes in some bleak hospital ward and finding Herbert Wehner praying over me.

Guillaume (*with* **Kretschmann**)   Let me go, Arno. Let me go home. You don't need me any more. What more do you want to know?

Kretschmann   Whether the treaties are going to be implemented. Whether Willy is going to survive long enough to make sure they are. You're closer to him than ever before, Günter! You practically live in his dispatch-case!

Guillaume   I could give Christel back her life. I could explain to Pierre.

Kretschmann   No more official cars, Günter! No more private train. No more upturned adoring faces. No more respectful attention from me at our little lunches. No more grateful appreciation from Mischa. No more sweet quiet Sundays, cruising out to the airport with Pierre. Or is it Willy you're worrying about?

Guillaume   If I resigned now he'd never find out about me. Let me go, Arno!

Kretschmann   We need you, Günter! We need you more than ever. Not just to tell us whether he's going to survive but to help him to. Who else can he depend upon, now that Ehmke's gone? Who else works the hours that you work? Never condemns him for his faults? Never takes offence at his indifference, or hurt at his slights? This is why *we* need you – because *he* needs you. Howl with him, Günter. Help him.

Wehner (*with* **Nollau**)   Guillaume?

Nollau   The name keeps jumping out of the files at us. Three separate espionage cases where Herr Guillaume seems to have known the defendants. So we looked up his birthday. The first of February. The date of the birthday greetings for G. I'm sorry to add to your troubles, which I know are legion.

Wehner   That's the complete case against him?

Nollau   So far.

Wehner   An initial and a date? And one son too many?

Nollau   We need more evidence. But getting more evidence means watching him. Leaving him in place and watching him.

Wehner   Make the big man look a bit small if it's true. He trusts him completely. Lets him see everything.

Nollau   Lets him see what? He *is* only union liaison? He won't be handling anything too sensitive?

Wehner   If they catch you hounding someone in Number One's office and you're wrong . . .

Nollau   They'll crucify me. Sorry, Herbert.

Wehner   You're in a difficult position, my friend.

Nollau   So how do we play this? What do we tell Willy?

Wehner   Nothing. We can't have him unsettled any further just at the moment. In any case he usually prefers to hear about problems after they've been solved.

Nollau   We can't just leave him in the dark! We'll have to tell him *something*!

Wehner   If we can't manage to be discreet we're going to find all kinds of nasty creatures coming out of the woodwork. Matters that we all hoped everyone had forgotten about.

Nollau   Oh, not that nonsense again! You don't really believe I committed a murder?

Wehner   Of course not.

Nollau   It was a pure fabrication! You know that!

Wehner   *I* know that.

Nollau   I was completely cleared!

Wehner   Let's keep you that way.

Nollau I'll have to tell Genscher, at any rate. My own Minister!

Wehner He'll immediately run bleating to Willy.

Nollau I'm sorry, but if I don't get Genscher's authorisation I'll be . . .

Wehner Crucified.

Nollau Crucified.

Wehner Question of how you put it. No need to go shouting 'Fire' at the top of your voice. Something more like a passing remark on the warmth of the weather. Then you're in the clear – and nobody panics.

Nollau They just get burnt to death.

Wehner Drawbacks to every policy.

Nollau And he *is* only union liaison . . .

Wilke (*with* **Brandt** *and* **Guillaume**)   Herr Wehner? Gone to East Berlin?

Brandt Private summit. Little chat with Honecker himself.

Wilke Prisoners and families?

Brandt Trying to get the trade going again.

Guillaume – Another unforeseen consequence of success. We normalise our relations – and it turns out that normal relations between two countries don't include buying and selling human beings.

Brandt I gather East Berlin's full of people sitting on their bags. They can't leave – they can't go back.

Guillaume – I don't know how much I've managed to find out about *this* country, but I've certainly found out a few things about my own.

Wilke When was this trip arranged, Herr Chancellor?

Brandt This afternoon, apparently. At an hour's notice. No unworthy suspicions, Reinhard! This is something he takes very seriously. The priest in him emerging from hiding once again.

Wilke With something of a rush.

Brandt He can scarcely have had time to pack the holy oil.

Guillaume – It *is* prisoners and families, is it, Arno?

Kretschmann – I've no idea.

Brandt Only another month, anyway, and we shall be on holiday. Out of all this mess. In the moist green depths of Norway, where remarkably little ever occurs.

Guillaume Nothing makes the Chancellor happier about being where he is than the prospect of being somewhere else.

Brandt No Uncle. No Helmut. No one at all except Uli to protect my privacy and Reinhard to intercept my messages.

Wilke I have a slight personal problem, Herr Chancellor. There is an unfortunate clash with the dates of my own family holiday.

Guillaume So who immediately steps forward to fill the breach?

Wilke Oh, I see . . . But *your* holiday, Herr Guillaume?

Guillaume Take it another time.

Wilke Your family, though . . .

Guillaume Glad to see the back of me! And the Chancellor and I are old travelling-companions.

Brandt Many a weary mile have I gone with Herr Guillaume at my side.

Kretschmann (*with* **Guillaume**)   You see? We all need you! We all depend upon you!

Guillaume   A whole month. Howling in the wilderness together.

Kretschmann   Where should *I* be without you? Back in East Berlin, eating Bratwurst in the office canteen! Where would *Mischa* be? You're the jewel in his crown, Günter! Even if you never told us anything, simply having you there at God's right hand would still be the justification of Mischa's whole career!

Brandt (*with* **Genscher**)   Guillaume? My little meatball?

Genscher   The usual nonsense. Nollau didn't even think it was worth mentioning to you. I said, 'Look, we can't have your people crawling round the Chancellor's office without getting his authorisation.'

Brandt   So what am I to do?

Genscher   Nothing. Carry on exactly as before. Nollau says not to change anything by a hairsbreadth.

Brandt   Same access to documents?

Genscher   Exactly the same.

Brandt   He's coming to Norway with me. He's going to have sole charge of all my communications with the outside world.

Genscher   Excellent chance for Nollau's people to watch him at work.

Brandt   I don't know where they can hide themselves. Middle of nowhere. Have to dress up as cows.

Genscher   Keep an eye on him yourself, perhaps.

Brandt   Provide a little entertainment. Nothing much else there to watch except the grass growing and Norwegian television.

Genscher   His wife's also under observation, incidentally.

Brandt   Whole family of spies!

Genscher   I don't know about their two sons.

Brandt   One son.

Genscher   Two, according to my information.

Brandt   One, according to Herr Guillaume.

Genscher   Nollau's obviously got the wrong man. In any case even the East Germans are hardly likely to be spying on someone who's just inscribed their wretched little state on the map of Europe for them.

Brandt   The merest possibility that Guillaume's not what he seems makes him infinitely more tolerable. (*With* **Guillaume**.) You have a moment, Herr Guillaume?

Guillaume   Chief. – Something odd about the way he's looking at me. As if I were someone else.

Brandt   Herr Guillaume, I've been having second thoughts about your kind offer to come to Norway with us.

Guillaume   – Genscher was here! Genscher's told him something!

Brandt   On reflection I feel it would be quite unforgivable of me to separate you from your family.

Guillaume   – I feel the wave of alarm go through me. And then the hollow behind the wave. Disappointment. Sheer childish disappointment. The party's over! He's never going to take me anywhere with him again!

Brandt   So why don't you bring them with you?

Guillaume   Why don't I . . . ? I'm sorry . . . ?

Brandt   Bring your wife! Christine, yes?

Guillaume   Christel.

Brandt   And your son. Pierre. Like my Peter. A great supporter of mine, I seem to remember. Rut and I will have one of our boys there. Not Peter – Matthias. Otherwise – perfect holiday symmetry. Us two and our son. You two and yours.

Guillaume   Chief, this is astonishingly kind . . .

Brandt   Pack your raincoats, Herr Guillaume. And a good supply of fresh jokes.

Kretschmann   – So you're happy again.

Guillaume   – He suddenly looks at you as if he's seen you for the first time. It's like a ray of sunlight striking down from the clouds, shining on you and you alone out of all the world. At once all the cold greyness of the day dissolves. You can feel the warmth in your bones.

Brandt   It *is* just the one boy?

Guillaume   Just the one, Chief.

Brandt   You should have persisted, Herr Guillaume. Two would have been even more fun.

Guillaume   – And it turns out to be the best family holiday we've ever had. They put us up in a charming little green wooden house just downhill from the Chief, and we all have the time of our life, all six of us. – Real holiday for Christel, Chief, yattering away to Rut. No idea where those two boys are, though. Vanished into the woods together again.

Brandt   Cops and robbers. Secret agents.

Guillaume   Getting on like a house on fire, anyway.

Brandt   Nice boy, your Pierre. You must be proud of him.

Guillaume   Light of my life.

Brandt   So different for them. Peace. Freedom.

Guillaume Fathers.

Brandt Who should we have turned out to be, if things had been different? You might have been standing here. I might have been standing there.

Guillaume Freedom, though. That's what's so relaxing about this place, Chief. You can leave all the doors unlocked and let the kids run wild.

Brandt You know why that is, Günter?

Guillaume Because the whole area's been sealed off by the local police.

Brandt Our own little police state to make you feel at home.

Guillaume – Time to think, time to talk. A little work, of course, at our respective jobs. Outgoing messages . . .

Brandt Negotiating points for Egon Bahr. Bit of a dog's breakfast. You'd better type them out before you send them.

Guillaume – Incoming telexes. Two copies of each. One for the Chief . . . – Personal message from Richard Nixon. – The other one for me. But we also spend hours out in the woods, like the boys, rambling around with Uli Bauhaus looking for mushrooms. (*With* **Bauhaus** *and* **Brandt**.) Makes a change to see you enjoying your work, Uli.

Bauhaus Makes a change to end up with some tangible results.

Brandt That's what I like about mushrooms, Uli. You pick them, you pickle them, you eat them; they stay picked, they stay pickled, they never try to eat you back. Spread them out on the table, then, and let's see what we've got. You're sloping off, are you, Günter? Not an initiate into the mycological mysteries?

Guillaume Too frightened of getting a wrong 'un.

Brandt   We can always spot a wrong 'un, can't we, Uli.

Guillaume   – So while the Chief and Uli sort their trophies I sort mine.

Bauhaus   Some real beauties.

Guillaume   – One or two quite attractive specimens.

Brandt   Sparassis. Rather uncommon.

Guillaume   – The British privately encouraging us to be nasty to the Americans.

Brandt   Wonderful sweet fragrance.

Guillaume   – Charmingly indiscreet tone.

Bauhaus   Look at this whopper!

Guillaume   – Oh, and a real corker here!

Brandt   Parasol. *Lepiota procera.*

Guillaume   – The French Foreign Minister in person, being even nastier about the Americans.

Brandt   Ask Rut to fry it in butter with a little chopped onion and chervil.

Guillaume   – Mischa should be able to cook up something rather tasty with this . . . I even get on well with Uli. In fact I get on well with the entire security team. Christel and I give a little drinks party for them, and Pierre takes snaps of them all. Then in the evening we stroll across and have drinks on the verandah with Willy and Rut.

Brandt   Fetch us out another couple of bottles, Uli. Then we shan't have to trouble you again.

Guillaume   – It's like one of those sessions in the office in the old days. Except there's no Uncle and no Helmut. Just Rut and Christel and the boys. Uli, waiting with gun in holster and corkscrew in hand. The Chief and me. Also one or two old friends who emerge from Willy's Norwegian past as the long northern twilight wears on.

Brandt   Willy Brandt isn't the only person I was when I was here in Norway in the thirties. I was also Willy Flamme. I was Karl Martin. I was Felix Franke. Each of them writing articles for a different paper, each of them with a slightly different viewpoint. You must learn English, Günter, and read Walt Whitman. 'Do I contradict myself? Very well then I contradict myself. I am large, I contain multitudes.'

Guillaume   Your first experience of presiding over a Cabinet, Chief.

Brandt   I must have been rather better at it then. I don't recall any major splits or betrayals. What about you? Being our good familiar Günter Guillaume can't have exhausted all your possibilities.

Guillaume   Only name I've ever had.

Brandt   People kept taking me for a spy. Not something anyone's ever accused you of?

Guillaume   Being a spy? No.

Brandt   The Norwegians thought I was spying for the Finns. The Swedes arrested me for spying for the Russians.

Guillaume   Can't see you as a spy.

Brandt   No?

Guillaume   Too noticeable. Too, if I may say so, Chief, secretive.

Brandt   I knew all the tricks of the trade. Learnt them when I was on the run from the Gestapo. Suitcases with false bottoms. Invisible ink.

Guillaume   Invisible ink? You have actually written messages in invisible ink?

Brandt   Useful training. It's what politicians do all the time. No, I could have been a spy, Günter. Might be one, for all you know. Might be spying now.

Guillaume   – And for a moment I wonder . . .

Kretschmann – Wonder what?

Guillaume – Nothing. Ridiculous. The Chief could no more spy than fly.

Brandt All right, it's 1936. Yes? For six months I'm back in Nazi Germany. In Berlin, working underground for the party. Who am I? Willy Brandt? Obviously not. Willy Flamme – Karl Martin – Felix Franke? No – I'm not even a German . . . May I introduce myself? My name is Gunnar Gaasland. I was born and brought up in Oslo, as I'm afraid is only too clear from my accent! A very exciting time to be in Berlin, and to see all the wonderful new political developments here!

Guillaume I believe you, Chief. Gunnar Gaasland, from Oslo!

Brandt And always, always, at the back of your mind, the fear that you'll be taken by surprise. Suddenly – another Norwegian. What will your Norwegian sound like to a Norwegian? – *Vi må sørge for å møtes en gang. Det ville være en lettelse å snakke norsk igjen noen timer . . .* ! – Will you pass or won't you? What if he's an old friend of Gunnar Gaasland's? Or what if you find yourself face to face with an old friend of Willy Brandt's? Or you're sitting talking with someone. Someone you've got to know quite well, perhaps. Feeling at ease with them. Feeling that everything's going well. And then you realise he's looking at you in a slightly odd way. At once you think . . .

Guillaume 'He knows!'

Brandt 'He knows . . . He knows . . .' It takes courage to live like that.

Guillaume I can imagine.

Brandt Courage and endurance.

Guillaume Yes.

Brandt More courage and endurance than I could muster. I fled, Günter. I fled. So perhaps you're right – I'm not a spy. Just a suitcase with a series of false bottoms. Willy Flamme, Karl Martin . . . Felix Franke, Gunnar Gaasland . . . And somewhere among them the most secret compartment of them all. The one that you can remember finding once, and that you can never quite find again.

Guillaume The one called Herbert Frahm.

Brandt Or is it someone else altogether? Another little boy. A rather cheerful, ordinary one, not solemn or serious at all. Someone rather like your Pierre. The little boy that Herbert Frahm might have been if his father had brought him up and told him stories and played with him. Or even acknowledged his existence and given him his name. Herbert Möller. The boy I might have been, and never was.

Guillaume – We sit there through the long Norwegian evenings, and in that unfamiliar northern light everything begins to seem strange and uncertain. I've become transparent to him, and he's playing with me, just as I am with him. Or is it only the possibility he's playing with? Or is that what I'm doing? Is it him I'm seeing in the half-light, or is it a reflection of myself?

Kretschmann – You're still handling the telexes?

Guillaume – Yes.

Kretschmann – And not being watched?

Guillaume – No.

Kretschmann – Certain?

Guillaume – Certain. Then one night he asks me the same question he asked me before.

Brandt And you still think I can trust them?

Guillaume – It's almost dark. I can't see the expression on his face. – I hope they haven't been listening in to some of the things you've been telling me, Chief, or they might start to have a few doubts about *you* . . .

Kretschmann – He can't see *your* face.

Guillaume – No. But in the end the time comes to leave, and I have to show you the collected fruits of all my labours. So I simply get two of our dispatch-cases . . .

Bauhaus These two?

Guillaume Thank you, Uli. – I pack up all my copies of the incoming and outgoing messages in *that* one, and put it in the boot of my car. *This* one I fill up with the little souvenirs that the Chief hands out on our travels. Then . . . – Uli!

Bauhaus If you're going to ask me to carry something back to Bonn for you . . .

Guillaume Classified documents, Uli.

Bauhaus I've got all the Chief's bags already. I've got five jars of pickled mushrooms.

Guillaume Uli, you're a trained security officer.

Bauhaus Yes. Not a porter.

Guillaume You're flying. I'm driving.

Bauhaus Certainly not *your* porter.

Guillaume Uli, if anything should happen to these papers while they were in the boot of my car . . .

Bauhaus It wouldn't be *my* responsibility.

Guillaume I'll tuck it under your arm, look. Now, don't let that box out of your sight, Uli. Not for an instant. Thanks, Uli. You're a pal.

Bauhaus I can't even draw my gun!

Guillaume If you need to draw your gun, Uli – drop the mushrooms. – And my fears are fully justified. We stop for

the night at a hotel in Sweden, and I lock the box of
souvenirs in our room while Christel and I go dancing. I
have a strong suspicion when we get back that somebody
has let themselves in and photographed the entire collection.

Kretschmann   – Worked like a charm. Thank you.

Guillaume   – So now we're back in the Palais
Schaumburg. And even if any suspicions crossed the Chief's
mind up there in Norway they've soon vanished into the
autumn mist, because everything's even worse than it was
before. There are wildcat strikes in the metalworking
industry. The dustmen aren't emptying the dustbins.

Kretschmann   – Sixty million Germanys!

Guillaume   – Helmut's raging away.

Schmidt   Someone's got to stand up to these people!
Someone's got to *do* something! Make some decisions! Give
this government a sense of purpose and direction!

Guillaume   – And where's Uncle off to?

Ehmke (*with* **Wilke** *and* **Guillaume**)   Can you believe he
actually said it? Even Herbert Wehner?

Wilke   'What the present German government lacks is a
head.'

Ehmke   At a press-conference! In *Moscow*, of all places!
We've only just established normal relations! The entire
world waiting to hear what he's going to say!

Wilke   'The Chancellor's asleep on his feet. He's lost in a
world of his own . . . Quite frankly I have never taken this
government seriously as a government . . .'

Ehmke   Who put him up to it, though? You know the
Russians are telling us in private that he's having more
secret meetings with his friends in East Berlin?

Wilke   What East Berlin is telling us in private is that the
Russians are lying.

Ehmke   Two old friends make a new friend – and at once they get jealous of each other. Another unforeseen consequence of our success. Life's such a tangle, Reinhard! Everyone looking at everyone else. Everyone seeing something different. Everyone trying to guess what everyone else is seeing. It's such an endless shifting unreliable indecipherable unanalysable *mess*!

Wilke   I think that what Herr Wehner is saying is comparatively simple. 'Sack me. Or sack yourself.'

Ehmke   And this time Willy will have to do it. He'll have to nerve himself to pick up the pistol and pull the trigger. It's either Willy or Uncle. They can't both survive.

Wehner (*with* **Ehmke**, **Wilke** *and* **Guillaume**) Banished! Exiled! Shut out from the sunshine of our great leader's smile!

Ehmke   Sacked?

Wehner   Sacked? Dear God, no. Made to sit in the corner at lunch. Firmness tempered with mercy, as always. The great peacemaker at work once again. Hands as unspotted as ever.

Ehmke (*with* **Wilke** *and* **Guillaume**)   So now of course it's Helmut's turn again to chisel away at him.

Schmidt (*with* **Brandt**)   'No.' That's the word, Willy. You must learn to say it! 'No . . . no . . . no . . .' They want a fifteen per cent pay rise? No. 'No' meaning no.

Brandt   'No' will mean no buses or trains, of course. No post. No hospitals.

Schmidt   It will also mean no lack of support from me as your Minister of Finance.

Guillaume   – So that's what he says. No. And what does it mean? It means no.

Ehmke   No buses or trains. No post. No hospitals. And no support from Helmut, because – no Helmut!

Wilke (*with* **Brandt**) He's in Washington, Herr
Chancellor.

Brandt And no word?

Wilke He says – just do whatever you think best.

Brandt Thank him, will you, Reinhard?

Ehmke (*with* **Guillaume**) So when the employers
collapse and 'no' turns out to mean 'yes', who's to blame?

Guillaume Willy.

Ehmke When the world's oil producers force prices up,
and suddenly there's no petrol in the pumps and no cars on
the autobahn, who's the guilty party?

Guillaume Willy.

Ehmke Who made the sun shine for them yesterday?

Guillaume Willy.

Ehmke So who's making it rain today?

Guillaume Willy.

Ehmke Who put the leak in their roof and the hole in
their shoe?

Guillaume Willy. Willy, Willy, Willy.

Ehmke He's dropped ten points in the polls. Even the
left-wing press have turned against him.

Kretschmann – Get him out of there, Günter. Get him
on the train again. More upturned faces. More smiling lips
and shining eyes. Make him happy again, Günter!

Guillaume (*with* **Brandt** *and* **Bauhaus**) Frimmersdorf
. . . Koblenz . . . Darmstadt . . . Suit pressed, clean shirt . . .
Who's who in Frimmersdorf, what's what in Darmstadt . . .
Uli – another bottle . . . ! Sign hanging in the cloakroom of
the Bundestag: Members Only. Scrawled across the bottom:
Also hats and coats . . . Neumarkt . . . Regensburg . . .

Also hats and coats . . . Neumarkt . . . Regensburg . . .
Straubing . . . A listener writes to Radio Yerevan: 'Is there
life on Mars?' Radio Yerevan replies: 'No, there is no life on
Mars, either . . .' Look at them out there, Chief! All those
faces gazing up from the darkness! Two words from you –
that's all they want! 'Dear friends . . . dear friends . . .!' No?
Look at *her*, then! The way her eyes are fixed on you! The
softness of her cheeks as she smiles! And those two women
further back. And more women, further back still, that you
can't quite see. And more again at the next station. So many
of them, Chief! So many different roads you could take!

Brandt   What have I done with my life, Günter? Moved
on, moved on. Adapted, adapted. Turned my back on
anyone who ever loved me. Forgotten anyone who ever
helped me on my way. Shed my skins, one after another,
like a snake . . . On and on the stations come. Plattling,
Vilshofen, Passau . . . Willy Flamme, Karl Martin, Felix
Franke . . . One face after another. One defeat after
another. And where do I end up? On a train, travelling
from nowhere to nowhere, to no point or purpose, making
my confession to Pastor Nobody.

Guillaume (*with* **Kretschmann**)   It doesn't work any
more, Arno. Not even the train. Then we're back in Bonn . . .
and there's another problem. They're tailing Christel.

Kretschmann   She's certain?

Guillaume   Certain.

Kretschmann   You want us to withdraw you?

Guillaume   Too late, now they're on to us. Everyone will
know it's true. A spy in Willy's own office! That really will
finish him. And anyway . . .

Kretschmann   *He'll* know.

Guillaume   Stupid, isn't it? He's going to know sooner or
later. And half of me longs to tell him!

Kretschmann   But face to face.

Guillaume   Not just run away, like a naughty little boy.

Kretschmann   You want to see the look in his eyes as he feels the knife go in.

Guillaume   I want him to see it was hard for me, as well as for him. Anyway, it may be a false alarm. Christel's up for a job in the Ministry of Defence. Routine check of some sort.

Kretschmann   Lie low for a bit. Take a holiday. Somewhere in the sun. Some place where the skies are blue all day. Wait and see.

Genscher (*with* **Brandt** *and* **Nollau**)   I understand that Herr Guillaume is out of the office today.

Brandt   Taking a well-deserved holiday.

Genscher   The best part of a year has gone by since you authorised Herr Nollau to place him under observation. I have been pressing Herr Nollau to tell me whether we now feel able to present the case for prosecution.

Brandt   Dear God, I assumed all that was long forgotten. Not that I ever saw the slightest sign of any activity. Your people are very skilled, Herr Nollau.

Nollau   Thank you, Herr Chancellor.

Brandt   You have actually found some evidence?

Nollau   We think so. We believe so. We feel we may have. On the other hand . . .

Genscher   Yes or no?

Nollau   Some difficulties and inconsistencies remain. One can imagine defence counsel making much of the second man, for example.

Genscher   The second man? What second man?

Nollau   In the original clandestine message on which the case would still largely depend. It referred, if you recall, to a second son.

Brandt   A second son? Or a second man?

Nollau   Let me see . . .

Genscher   Oh, no! Oh, for heaven's sake!

Nollau   'Congratulations on the second man.'

Genscher   The second *man* in the family is the son!

Nollau   I see. Of course. So the first man is . . . ?

Brandt   Resting from his labours.

Guillaume (*with* **Kretschmann**)   I set off before dawn for the long drive south. I glance in my mirror as I turn out of the petrol station, and there, in the first grey light, is a car waiting on the hard shoulder about three hundred metres behind me. I move off. He moves off. I turn onto the autobahn. He turns onto the autobahn. I hit a steady 120. He stays sitting in my mirror. Across the frontier into Belgium and he's still there. On into France, and he holds 160 with me all the way to Paris. My own personal assistant! As faithful to me as I am to Willy. Then at Fontainebleau the French police take over . . .

Kretschmann   They let you have your holiday?

Guillaume   My last holiday. In the south. In the sun.

Kretschmann   You thought of staying there? Of never coming back?

Guillaume   Every sunlit hour of every sunlit day. The simple life. A glass of wine on a shaded terrace. The scent of rosemary and thyme. All thought jammed out by the cicadas . . .

Kretschmann   Your life's work done.

Guillaume   At peace with the world around me. My own simple self at last. Not even my own self. No one.

Kretschmann   You could have gone home. Now you knew you were blown. You could have crossed back to the East.

Guillaume   They gave me the chance. They followed me north as far as Fontainebleau. Then this afternoon – nothing. All the way to the border – no one. Petrol in the tank. Money in my pocket.

Kretschmann   Why didn't you? Pierre?

Guillaume   Also Christel.

Kretschmann   And your current lady-friend.

Guillaume   You. Mischa.

Kretschmann   Willy, of course.

Guillaume   Such an ignominious exit. I don't want him to remember me like that.

Kretschmann   Our last meeting, then?

Guillaume   Looks like it.

Kretschmann   Four years, though!

Guillaume   Not bad.

Kretschmann   One for the history books, Günter. In the chapter on Willy Brandt you'll always have your paragraph.

Knocking. Darkness. Doorbell. A crack of light.

Voice   Herr Günter Guillaume?

Guillaume   Yes?

Voice   We have a warrant for your arrest.

The crack of light opens to the width of a door.

Nollau (*with* **Brandt** *and* **Guillaume**)   Half-past six this morning, Herr Chancellor. At his flat. His wife was also arrested.

Brandt   And Pierre. Their son. Was he present? Did he see it happen?

Nollau   I believe he came out of his bedroom while the arrest was being made. I'm pleased to say Guillaume confessed at once.

Guillaume   I am a citizen of East Germany, and one of its officers. I must ask you to respect that.

Brandt   A citizen of East Germany. One of its officers . . . He gave you the case. You wouldn't have had one otherwise. He sentenced himself.

Nollau   I realise that a number of mistakes have been made in the course of this investigation, Herr Chancellor. I hope you feel it has now been pursued to a satisfactory conclusion.

Brandt   He did it for Pierre. He betrayed me – and then he betrayed his other master as well. To explain to Pierre.

Nollau   Perhaps also to explain to you, Herr Chancellor.

Guillaume (*alone, sits*)   Sorry, Arno. The only time I dropped my guard in all the eighteen years I've spent here. The only mistake I made . . . I wonder where *you* are now? Vanished into the mist, I hope . . . Strange – *you* can see *me*. Gazing out at you from every newspaper and television screen in West Germany. You can guess what I'm doing, too. Reporting to you still! Inside my head. Telling you everything! Telling you sorry. Telling you I know I let Mischa down.

Brandt (*with* **Ehmke**)   Trust no one. That's the miserable lesson of these last four years.

Ehmke   Not even me. I hired him. I vetted him. Not even you. For a whole year you've known he was under surveillance. And not a word of warning to me.

Brandt   What kind of man must he be, though? What kind of people are they who sent him? You're robbed by the beggar you befriend, and you feel ashamed for him. Ashamed for yourself, too, for trusting him.

Guillaume   – And Willy. I let Willy down. I saw him on the news. He looked sick at heart. His first trip without me to watch over him. Wearing half of one suit and half of another! And no upturned faces! Who wrote his schedule? Who sent him on a walkabout when everyone was at home watching the football?

Wilke (*with* **Ehmke**)   All the journalists are complaining. One of them said: 'It was never like this when Günter was organising it.' Meanwhile there's Willy, standing on a clifftop, gazing into the depths below.

Brandt   – If you're going to fall, where's the better place to land? In the soft swamp of disgrace, to flounder helplessly on? Or on the hard ground, with all your struggles over? One long moment of terror, and then such . . . such simplicity.

Ehmke (*with* **Wilke** *and* **Brandt**)   Come on, Willy. We can soon fix this. All it needs is for me to go on television and say that at every stage in Guillaume's career the proper vetting and security procedures were followed.

Wilke   They weren't.

Ehmke   You're not the one who's going to say it.

Brandt   If only I hadn't given up smoking.

Ehmke   So, Willy, your great reshuffle. What are you going to do with Helmut? He wants the Foreign Ministry, and so does Genscher.

Brandt   Such a shabby way to go. Such an ignominious exit.

Ehmke   Leave it all to me, Willy. I'll fix it. We'll have you chancelling again in no time.

Nollau (*with* **Bauhaus**)   The women? What women?

Bauhaus   On the train. On his travels.

Nollau   Oh, I see. I don't think this is in any way relevant to our inquiries, Herr Bauhaus.

Bauhaus   I'm sorry. I thought I should mention it.

Nollau   There's no secret about Herr Brandt's weakness in this direction.

Bauhaus   Anyway, I've given your people the list if you need it . . .

Nollau   You made a list?

Bauhaus   Part of my job – check his visitors. I couldn't always get their names. Time in and time out, though. And some kind of rough indication of the different categories. Journalists, party workers, and so on. Local supporters, prostitutes . . .

Nollau   I don't think we need to pursue this any further, Herr Bauhaus.

Bauhaus   No, only I just thought, if Herr Guillaume was keeping a list as well . . .

Nollau   Guillaume? *Guillaume* knew about Herr Brandt's proclivities?

Bauhaus   When we were on the train. Herr Guillaume had to help me . . . well . . .

Nollau   Help you what?

Bauhaus   Control the queue. And I just thought, if he'd given the list to his people in East Berlin . . .

Nollau   So . . . Journalists, you say? Party workers? What kind of numbers are we talking about . . . ?

Guillaume   – The women! Suddenly it's the only thing my interrogators are interested in! But everyone knew! Everyone's always known! Why have people suddenly started to talk about it?

Genscher (*with* **Brandt**)   I hardly need say that I find this an intensely distasteful task. I knew as soon as Nollau put it in my hands, though, that I had no choice but to show it to you.

Guillaume   – It wasn't me, Arno! Not a word have I said! Not me, Chief! Not me!

Genscher   Every single time we sit down to negotiate with them, whatever it's about – trade, refugees, border controls – we'll know they're holding this behind their backs.

Brandt   Pure nonsense, of course. For the most part. Sadly. Rather flattering, though, for a man of my age.

Wehner (*with* **Schmidt**)   We've put a knife in their hands.

Schmidt   One in *your* hands as well, of course . . .

Wehner   Not a weapon I should have chosen.

Schmidt   This list. It's in your handwriting.

Wehner   Nollau read it aloud to me.

Schmidt   And you took it down? At dictation? All ten pages?

Wehner   Old journalist – I write shorthand. I'm sorry it should have happened like this, Helmut. I know how distasteful you find it.

Schmidt   Every encounter. Every category of woman at every stop along the line. In shorthand.

Wehner   Helmut, we both always knew he'd have to go in the end. It was only a question of when he became more of a liability than an asset to the party.

Bauhaus (*with* **Brandt**)   I'm sorry, Chief. I know you feel I've let you down.

Brandt   *I'm* sorry. I seem to have given you an inordinate amount of labour.

Bauhaus   They kept on and on at me! I got confused! I'm an ordinary family man. I was out of my depth. Chief, I've served you faithfully for four years! Day in, day out! Fetched and carried for you! And always ready, at the slightest sudden movement in the corner of my eye, to step between you and the gun!

Brandt   And all the time there was another Uli there, waiting to emerge from the shadows when the moment came.

Schmidt (*with* **Wehner**)   We'll all have to give him our support, of course.

Wehner   Of course. Our full support.

Schmidt   You'll make that clear to him?

Wehner   Don't worry, Helmut. Your hands will be clean. Just as Number One's always were.

Guillaume   – The Chief knows he can rely on me! He knows we'd never try to undermine him! That's not what we meant at all!

Wehner (*with* **Brandt**)   The choice is obviously yours. You could resign the chancellorship, but stay on as party chairman – or you could give up the party as well.

Brandt   You've seen Nollau's list?

Wehner   I didn't note the details.

Brandt   Pity. They would have amused you.

Wehner   Or you could try to struggle on. Whatever you decide, you know I'll stand behind you.

Brandt   Where you have always stood.

Wehner   Precisely where I have always stood.

Brandt   With Helmut beside you.

Wehner   And if you do decide to hang on then you can count on us both to support you in exactly the same way as we always have.

Brandt   It's helpful to know that one has some friends one can rely upon not to change.

Wehner   Shall I ask Helmut to join us?

Brandt   So many people, with so many different views and so many different voices. And inside each of us so many more people still, all struggling to be heard. For a moment one voice rises above the others, and everyone picks up the tune. And then the cacophony resumes. Until sooner or later another voice is raised . . .

Wehner   Helmut! (*With* **Brandt** *and* **Schmidt**.) I think Number One has reached a decision.

Schmidt   I felt I should wait until you'd made up your own mind. I shouldn't like anyone to think I'd attempted to influence you. Let me merely say that, whatever your decision is . . .

Brandt   I have your support.

Schmidt   My unswerving support.

Brandt   Thank you. I think I can see a way of doing it that would enable me to offer you the Foreign Ministry.

Schmidt   Offer me the . . . ?

Brandt   Foreign Ministry. Isn't that what you want? When I reshuffle? Keep Genscher out of it, at any rate. I'm going to make a completely fresh start. Get rid of Grabert. Bring in someone else to run the Chancellor's office.

Schmidt   I see. You're not . . . ?

Brandt   Not what?

Schmidt   I thought . . . Herbert thought . . .

Wehner   I think even Number One thought.

Brandt   Thought, yes. Thought and thought. Decided even. But what voice will speak when you open your mouth you never know for certain until it does.

Schmidt   So . . . Well . . . Of course . . .

Brandt   Not even *you*.

Schmidt   No . . . Only . . . Well . . .

Brandt   Will you fight or will you run? Who knows until the moment comes? And since I have your support. Your unswerving support . . .

Bauhaus (*with* **Nollau**)   One other possibility I should mention. Guillaume may also have had well . . . photos.

Nollau   More photos?

Bauhaus   He was a professional photographer.

Nollau   So?

Bauhaus   When we were on the train he had the compartment adjoining the Chief's . . .

Wilke (*with* **Wehner** *and* **Schmidt**)   No more than one might expect from the gutter press, of course. I thought you'd better see it, though.

Wehner   'Did Brandt Spy Take Sex Photos?'

Schmidt   Where did this one come from?

Wehner   No idea.

Wilke   Have you seen him today? He looks just about at the end of his tether.

Wehner   Been up all night, I gather. Drinking. Wavering. Muttering about pistols and high cliffs . . .

Brandt *joins them.* **Wilke** *gives him the newspaper.*

Wilke   I'm sorry to be the messenger . . .

Brandt   So many people eager to lend a helping hand.

Schmidt   But where did they get the story?

Guillaume   – Not from me, Chief! No story – no photographs! You know that!

Brandt (*to* **Wehner**)   I never asked how your meeting went. With your friends in East Berlin on Friday.

Wehner   Fruitful, I think.

Brandt   Prisoners and families?

Wehner   Not this time.

Brandt   No?

Wehner   Economic co-operation. Long-planned. As you know.

Brandt   So much support . . . You open your mouth to surrender, and you hear a voice saying: 'I'm damned if I will!' You open it again, and this time it's another voice altogether. Saying: 'Done for. Finished. Sunk.' Well . . . Various people I shall have to inform first, of course. My family. The party. Our coalition partners. My official letter of resignation Grabert can take to the President this evening. (*To* **Schmidt**.) I know that Herbert will give you exactly the same kind of support as he has always given me.

Schmidt   Willy, stop. Stop, stop, stop. Let's all just pause and think for a moment. Let's not get ourselves rushed into a decision we might all regret. Willy . . .!

Wehner (*with* **Schmidt** *and* **Wilke**)   I shouldn't get too excited. He'll change his mind a few more times yet.

Schmidt   One of us must go after him, stop him, reason with him!

Wehner   Don't worry. It's me they'll point the finger at, not you.

Schmidt   We can't survive without Willy! I'll never carry the party! They love him!

Wehner   They'll love you, too. In time. If you feed them and keep them warm. If I'm there to be hated. If love is what you want.

Schmidt   I can't do it, Herbert! Not like this!

Wehner   He was right about one thing. Fight or run? Pull the trigger or drop the gun? Not one of us who knows which it will be until it's happened.

Ehmke (*with* **Schmidt**, **Wehner** *and* **Wilke**)   Where's Willy? I think I may have swung it! Went on television and really did my stuff. Said we'd done all the security checks in the world. Done them ten times over. Lied and lied until I believed it myself . . . Where is he?

Wehner   Resigning.

Ehmke   I knew it.

Wehner   Or not resigning.

Wilke *gives* **Ehmke** *the newspaper.*

Wehner   In two minds about it. Making up both of them.

Ehmke   Someone should go and make sure he's all right.

Schmidt   You, presumably.

Ehmke   Strange, isn't it. Everybody loves him – and nobody does he have to turn to. Nobody in the whole wide world.

Schmidt   He has you.

Ehmke   Not even me.

Guillaume (*alone*)   The nobody he turned to once was me. An upturned face like all the others that he spoke to from his heart. The upturned face for ever at his side. The smiling face with nothing behind it. No secret ambitions, no concealed disagreements, no hidden resentments. He didn't like me much. He told Horst Ehmke to get rid of me.

The expectant murmur of an audience.

Told him to, but never made him do it.

Handbell. Silence.

Woman's voice   Ladies and gentlemen, I declare the result of the vote to be as follows. Those in favour: 267. Those against: 225.

Applause. Lights up on Schmidt.

I therefore declare, according to article 63 paragraph 2 of the Basic Law, that the proposed Member has received the votes of the majority of Members of the Bundestag. Herr Schmidt, I must ask you if you accept election as Chancellor of the Federal Republic of Germany.

Guillaume   – His faithful nobody. And just when he needed me most I wasn't there.

Schmidt   Frau President, I accept the election.

Guillaume   I think about it all over the years as I serve my long sentence, and I see just how the pieces in the puzzle fall into place. The distrust, the jealousy. The economics, the illness. Schmidt and Wehner. Nollau and Genscher and Bauhaus. Herbert Frahm and Herbert Möller. And finally me. I've let myself be used! Not just by Mischa. Not just by you, Arno. By Herbert Wehner. That's what burns. I've been picked up by Wehner, like a handy lump of wood by a murderer, and used to club Willy down. Not for one

moment do I let anyone see my shame. But ashamed I am,
Arno! Ashamed at last . . .

Kretschmann   – Nothing I can do for you now but
count the days of your sentence off with you one by one,
while we wait for Mischa to get you exchanged. Six years it
takes us before we manage to bring you home.

Guillaume   Home, yes. Only I've got cancer by this time.
I've lost all contact with Pierre.

Kretschmann (*with* **Guillaume**)   Thirty prisoners we
paid for you, Günter! You always wanted to know if it was
true about the prisoners. And the price has gone up.
They're worth almost a hundred thousand marks a head
now. Three million marks we valued you at!

Guillaume   Home. Is it? I see it with very different eyes
now. And how thin that single voice sounds once your ears
have got attuned to the complexity of counterpoint! In any
case you were right. Now Willy had made peace with the
Russians they didn't need to keep their wretched little ally
on its feet any longer.

The faint thudding of a pickaxe.

(*with everyone.*) That knocking in the timbers grows louder
and louder as the months and years go by – and it turns out
that this is where the noise was coming from all the time.
Not that house. The house next door. Our house.

Brandt   The journalists rang me in the middle of the
night to get my reaction. The event we'd waited so long for
has actually begun to happen. The state whose existence I
recognised is passing out of existence before our eyes. The
point of all that suffering and struggle and deception is
crumbling into dust.

*The single pickaxe is joined by more. The sound grows louder. Everyone
rises and gazes out into the house. The thudding of the pickaxes
culminates in the rumble of collapsing masonry. Light.*

And at last what belongs together is coming together. Our divided self has become one self.

Guillaume   The old peacemaker sets out on his travels once again. So many new lands to wander! So many more upturned faces!

Brandt   Eisenach and Dresden . . . Leipzig and Rostock . . .

Guillaume   All wanting to see the man who first began to make this happen. Does he ever miss me organising the timetables and laying out his suit? Does he ever consider that I played my own small part in all this? The little man who looked at the great man, and saw that he could be trusted.

Brandt   I sometimes wonder about him, of course. His son's turned his back on him, his homeland's vanished. We're both mortally ill.

Guillaume   I watch him as he passes. He's changed. So have I. So has everyone and everything. Herbert Wehner . . .

Wehner   Dead and with the angels.

Guillaume   Helmut Schmidt . . .

Schmidt   Long since out of office.

Ehmke   And our great party with him.

Guillaume   Hans-Dietrich Genscher, who could never be Foreign Minister . . .

Genscher   Foreign Minister for the last fifteen years.

Guillaume   And where are you, Arno? Vanished again before they arrest you. Melted into the crowd, like so many others.

Kretschmann   – I stand among them and cheer with all the rest as Willy passes. Cheer with all my heart. A great man!

Brandt   We're healed and whole. For a little while, at any rate. And for a little while everyone's glad.

Guillaume   And wherever he goes, my shadow goes with him. Together still.

Darkness.

POSTSCRIPT

Nineteen seventy-two marked the high summer of Willy Brandt's brief but remarkable career as German Chancellor. It was also, as it happened, the year in which I made my first serious visit to Germany, and first became fascinated by it – particularly by its evolution since the Second World War. Perhaps this is why the complex and painful story of Brandt's downfall two years later captured my imagination at the time, and has been lurking at the back of my mind ever since.

Brandt was one of the most attractive public figures of the twentieth century, who won people's trust and love not only in Germany but all over the world. He first became a national and international celebrity in the 1950s, when he was Governing Mayor of West Berlin, and led the city's resistance to the efforts of the Soviet Union to undermine and intimidate it so that it could be absorbed into the East German state surrounding it. After his resignation from the Federal Chancellorship in 1974 he won himself a completely new reputation with yet another career as an internationalist and champion of the Third World. His greatest achievements, though, were in Federal politics. The first of them was to help reform his party, the SPD (the Social Democrats), so as to make it electable by the cautiously conservative German voters. The second was single-handedly to seize the chance, when it was at last offered by a modest improvement in the party's share of the vote in 1969, of forming an SPD-led coalition – the first left-of-centre coalition in Germany, with the first left-of-centre Chancellor, since Hitler had crushed parliamentary democracy in the early thirties. His real triumph, though, was the use to which he put the power he had gained: to secure what had hitherto seemed a politically impossible goal – a reconciliation with Germany's former enemies in Eastern Europe.

The difficulty was that this could be done only by at last recognising the painful realities created by the outcome of the war. One of these was the loss of nearly a quarter of

Germany's territory in the East. The other was the existence
within the remaining German lands of the second state that
had grown out of the Soviet zone of occupation – the
German Democratic Republic, alien in its political
character, bound hand and foot to the Soviet instead of the
Western power bloc, and sealed off behind closed frontiers
that sundered all natural family and social connections.
There was entrenched and embittered opposition to
accepting either fact, particularly from those most directly
involved – the 8 million Germans who had been expelled
from the former German territories east of the Oder and
Neisse rivers, which had now been divided up between the
Soviet Union and Poland, plus the 4 million who had fled
from East Germany, and the millions more who had
relatives still trapped there. But Brandt succeeded in doing
it, and succeeded totally. The consequences of this
reconciliation reached far beyond Germany. They changed
the face of Europe, and of the world, by making possible the
gradual scaling down of the Cold War – and thereby,
eventually, an event that Brandt never foresaw: the end of
the very state whose existence he had recognised, followed
by the collapse of the entire Soviet empire.

   In the summer of 1972, when I arrived in Germany,
Brandt's government was in the middle of this great work.
In spite of the severe difficulties it was encountering at home
because of its small and steadily vanishing majority in the
Bundestag, it was already ratifying the treaties it had
negotiated with the Soviet Union and Poland. I can't say
that I paid very much attention to these triumphs at the
time. Federal politics happened in Bonn, and Germany for
me that summer was Berlin, the once-great city I had come
to Germany to write about, now only notionally the capital,
left marvellous but functionless deep inside East Germany,
like a luxury liner that had somehow become beached in the
sandy wastes of the Mark Brandenburg.

   The city compelled the imagination in all kinds of ways.
Its greatest fascination, though, was undoubtedly its greatest
monstrosity – the Wall, the hideous concrete barrier,
enforced by armed guards and a complex series of lethal

mantraps, that the East German government had been forced to erect in 1961 to stop the massive haemorrhage of its citizens to the West. Another much longer wall, from the Baltic to Thuringia, divided the German Democratic Republic from West Germany proper, but the Berlin Wall obtruded more on the consciousness because it closed in the Western half of the city as tightly as the fence round a suburban garden. Wherever you went you came face to face with it barring the street you were in, and defining the geography of Berlin even more sharply than the Hudson river does the geography of New York.

Somewhere out of sight behind it that summer Egon Bahr and Michael Kohl, the representatives of the Federal and Democratic German Republics respectively, were negotiating the terms of the Basic Treaty by which the West was at last to recognise the East, and by which relations between the two states were at last to be given some semblance of normality. Already a new agreement on Berlin itself, signed by the four former allies, was for the first time making it possible for West Berliners to visit the Eastern half of their city. Friends of mine came back to the modern wonderland of West Berlin stunned by the different kind of wonderland that they had found on the other side of the Wall: cobbled streets, unlit villages, pockmarked tenements, snorting steam trains – the long-lost old Germany of the Weimar Republic and the Third Reich, magically preserved in all its nostalgic dullness and shabbiness, as if in some vast grey heritage park, by the conservatism of the Communists and the backwardness of their economy.

The existence of this other Germany, and the endless puzzle of its relations with the Federal Republic, was part of what made modern German politics the most interesting in Europe. How even to refer to it officially without seeming to acknowledge that it was a separate state? The right-wing press stuck with 'the Soviet Zone', or even simply 'the Zone', long after it had acquired a government of its own. The usual official euphemism was 'the other part of Germany'. Kiesinger, Brandt's predecessor as Chancellor, described it not as a state but a 'phenomenon'. Brandt was prepared to concede that it was a state, but refused to see it as a foreign one. As he famously said, in the statement of his new government's policies in 1969: 'Even if two states exist in Germany they are not foreign to each other; their relations to each other can only be of a special sort.'

Whatever West Germans called it, there were endless practical difficulties in coping with a hostile next-door neighbour that was obsessed with spying on every aspect of life, not only internally but externally – particularly since all its 15 million citizens were potential agents because they spoke exactly the same language – and since a further 4 million of them were inside the gates already. What could such close cousins, who found themselves upon such different paths in life, make of each other? How would they behave as their relationship began to change?

The complexities of the situation were made painfully personal in the story of Willy Brandt and Günter Guillaume. Guillaume, who had crossed over from East Berlin thirteen years earlier, joined the Chancellor's office as a junior aide within weeks of Brandt's election in 1969. For the next four years he served Brandt with devotion and efficiency, and rose to become the personal assistant who organised his travels and accompanied him wherever he went. He was also spying on him, it turned out, with equal devotion and efficiency, on behalf of his employers in the East German Ministry of State Security, and his arrest in 1974 precipitated Brandt's resignation.

Exactly why it did, though, is by no means obvious. In his official letter of resignation Brandt said that he assumed political responsibility for negligence in connection with the affair. The security services had indeed committed a catalogue of errors in failing to vet Guillaume properly before his appointment, and in allowing him to continue even after the first serious suspicions had been raised against him. In private some of Brandt's colleagues told him that he was open to blackmail by the East German government, because Guillaume had presumably supplied them with a list of Brandt's extra-marital activities. But historians tend to agree that the unmasking of Guillaume was more the occasion of the Chancellor's downfall than its cause. It took its place among a complex of factors arising from the political situation inside the Federal Republic, from the internal conflicts of the SPD and its leaders, from Brandt's own character and physical condition – even from the very success that he had achieved.

Peter Merseburger, Brandt's most recent biographer, mocks supporters of Brandt who detect treachery and see his fall as a kind of regicide. 'As if, in the respectable republican court at Bonn there had been Shakespearean dramas, opponents are demonised as Brutus-figures who carried daggers under their robes, even as dark Nibelung warriors who had nothing in mind but to assassinate the Chancellor's character.' Politics, as Merseburger says, is mostly 'terribly banal', and the events of 1974 were no exception. Among the banalities, nevertheless, were many strands of powerful personal feeling, of loyalty and jealousy, of courage and despair. It was really the sheer complexity of this mixture that finally decided me to write the play. Complexity is what the play is about: the complexity of human arrangements and of human beings themselves, and the difficulties that this creates in both shaping and understanding our actions.

*

The only part of German history that seems to arouse much interest in the British is the Nazi period. That brutal holiday from the moral restraints under which West European societies normally labour possesses a kind of corrupt glamour for even the most timid and law-abiding. The half-century that has followed Germany's awakening from the sick dream is thought to be a time of dull respectability, with the Federal Republic characterised by nothing much except material prosperity, and formed in the image of the peaceful and provincial Rhineland town which was the seat of its government for most of the period.

To me, I have to say, that material prosperity, that peacefulness, even that supposed dullness, represent an

achievement at which I never cease to marvel or to be
moved. It's difficult to think of parallels for such an unlikely
political, economic and moral resurgence. What other
nation, even Japan, has risen so swiftly from beginnings as
abject as the physical ruin, moral degradation and political
paralysis in which Germany found itself in 1945? Federal
Germany began life as a graveyard in which almost every
city had been reduced to rubble, and almost every
institution and political resource contaminated by
complicity in the crimes of National Socialism; yet from this
utter desolation, without recourse to despotism or military
means, its citizens constructed one of the most prosperous,
stable, and decent states in Europe, the cornerstone of a
peace which has endured now, at least in Western Europe,
for nearly sixty years.

The process was greatly assisted, it's true, by some of the
consequences of defeat itself. It was in the first place the
presence of the occupying armies that probably saved
Germany from the revolutions and counter-revolutions by
which it was ravaged after the First World War. Then there
were the refugees from the East. By 1950 nearly 8 million of
the 12 forced out of the lost provinces of East Prussia and
the Sudetenland flooded into the Western zones of
occupation. How the shattered country ever absorbed them
beggars the imagination. A further 3 million arrived over
the years, plus another 4 million from East Germany. This
flood of immigrants, though, provided the Federal Republic
with the labour it needed to rebuild. Recovery was also
helped by Marshall Aid, provided to the Western zones of
occupation by America even while the Russians were still
pillaging their own zone (though the net value of it, when
offset against reparations and occupation costs, has been
queried by some historians; and in any case Germany
received less of it than Britain and other European
countries).

Even the famous currency reform of 1948, which gave
birth to the mighty Deutschmark, and which first kicked the
moribund economy into life again, was sprung upon
Germans not by Ludwig Erhard, their economics minister,

as is generally supposed, but by the Americans (and hijacked by Erhard in a spectacular double-double-cross which would provide the material for another play). The currency reform also precipitated the splitting of the nation, because the Soviet Union refused to accept the Deutschmark in its zone of occupation. But this, too, had its positive effects for West Germany, because it marked a further step in the division of the entire world into two competing empires, whose confrontation in the ensuing cold war swiftly transformed America's defeated enemy into its crucial front-line ally.

German politicians were reluctant to endorse the dismemberment of their nation, and the concept of West Germany as a separate political entity seems to have originated once again with the Americans (according to Dean Acheson, it was first proposed by the US Military Governor, General Lucius Clay). The new state even acquired the constitution that has served it so well ever since (more properly called the Basic Law, so as not to imply any constitutional acceptance of the country's division) only because it was instructed by the occupying powers to compose one.

In the end, though, the success of the new state was created by the efforts of its own citizens – by the sheer hard labour of its workers, by the crafts that were lying dormant in people's fingertips and the professional and entrepreneurial skills in their brains, by the readiness of so many people to put the public good at least as high as their own personal profit – and by the political skills of the leaders it found. The Basic Law was signed into effect, and the first Federal election held, in 1949, but there was already a complex political landscape in place: the *Länder*, the patchwork of provinces that make up the German nation (eleven of them at the time), together with their governments. Their heterogeneity reflects the very different characters and histories of the various German states that were assembled to compose Imperial Germany in 1871, and the combination of their individual politics with their participation in the Federal politics of Bonn created the characteristic complexity of modern German politics.

Since that first election in 1949, which brought the wily Konrad Adenauer to power, the Federal government has gone through many crises and scandals. It has survived many revelations that its members or officers had been implicated in the crimes of the past, or were working for East German intelligence, and many alarms when the nationalistic right seemed to be resurgent, or when the electorate seemed to be still nostalgic for past glories. In the last decade the longed-for reunification with the Eastern *Länder* has plunged the nation into its most severe and prolonged difficulties yet. But the Federal Republic has worked. It has proved stable and moderate. It has even survived its dependence upon coalition as a way of life – something which appears unworkable to British and American eyes, which has caused endemic weakness in France and Italy, and which indeed destroyed the Weimar Republic and opened the door to Hitler. Every West German government since the Federal Republic was founded has been a coalition, usually between the CDU/CSU (the conservative alliance formed by the Christian Democratic Union of the northern *Länder* and the Christian Social Union of Bavaria) on the one hand and the tiny FDP, the Free Democratic Party (aka the Liberals) on the other.

In 1966, though, coalition politics reached its bizarre apotheosis in the so-called Grand Coalition, when the junior partner of the CDU/CSU became not the FDP but the SPD, their principal antagonist, hitherto apparently doomed to serve as the permanent Opposition. Willy Brandt was bounced into the arrangement against his wishes by his colleagues Herbert Wehner and Helmut Schmidt, because the plane bringing him from Berlin to the crucial meeting was delayed by fog. But, once again, the arrangement worked. Brandt himself, with his charm, his fluency in other languages, and his impeccable political past, made a natural Foreign Minister. And although he loathed Georg Kiesinger, the CDU Chancellor and a former member of the Nazi Party, to the point where he claimed to feel physically ill in his presence, the coalition lasted for three years, and is regarded by some commentators as one of the most successful governments in the history of the Federal Republic.

The elections in the autumn of 1969 transformed the politics of coalition once again. Although it still trailed the Christian Democrats, the SPD picked up enough seats to raise the possibility of securing a slim majority in the Bundestag by going into coalition with the FDP. Wehner and Schmidt were against it; they wanted to continue with the existing arrangement. With entirely uncharacteristic decisiveness, Brandt seized his chance. Wehner and Schmidt had bounced him into the Grand Coalition; now he bounced them out of it. Without a word to either of them he went on television on election night and announced that he would seek to form a new government with the FDP. He succeeded, and three weeks later the new Bundestag elected him Chancellor.

Which is where my play begins.

*

Two mutually contradictory developments had conspired to bring the SPD and the electorate somewhat closer together. The first was the change in the nature of the party that had begun at its conference in Bad Godesberg ten years earlier, when Brandt, Wehner and Schmidt had persuaded it to dump its residual Marxism in favour of the so-called social market economy. The second was the change in the nature of the electorate brought about by the events on the streets of Germany in the previous year.

The 'student movement' of 1968 swept all the way across Europe and the USA. But it had begun the year before in Berlin. The trigger was a demonstration against a visit by the Shah of Persia, and its heavy-handed suppression by the police, during which they shot and killed a student called Benno Ohnesorg. The wave of demonstrations, strikes and sit-ins that ensued all over the world was like the long-stored energy released in an earthquake. It came from a huge idealism that had found little outlet in the cautious compromises of parliamentary democracy. In Germany there were two additional causes of frustration. One was the new generation's realisation that the apparently solid fabric of German society rested upon foundations built out of the rubble of its National Socialist past, and which were by unspoken common consent not to be inspected too closely. The second was the extreme expression of the consensuality of post-war German politics in the Grand Coalition, which left all the functions of an Opposition to the tiny, impotent and far from radical FDP.

So the radical left had constituted itself as an informal 'extra-parliamentary Opposition'. This chaotic grouping was, needless to say, far more disparate than any official coalition could ever be, and it was the spectacular array of its fission products that caught my eye when I arrived in Berlin in 1972. Some of its factions were rigidly subservient to the SED (the 'Socialist Unity Party' that ruled East Germany), some of them were Maoist, some of them nostalgic throwbacks to the KPD, the old Communist Party of the Weimar years, some of them engaged in increasingly brutal terrorism. A wide range of idealistic lifestyles and business enterprises had sprung up in the city, a kaleidoscope of 'left-oriented' communes, of pubs and cafés selling drinks and hot cakes at 'comrades' prices'.

The movement produced a sympathetic shift to the left among many voters who were never part of it. A number of its most active and effective adherents, in any case, decided to pursue their battle within the framework of practical politics. They proclaimed 'the long march through the institutions', including the unions and the SPD, with the intention of bringing them under their control by constitutional means. All this helped to earn the party the small increase in its vote in 1969 (3.4 per cent) that put it within reach of real power. The pressures it produced inside the party, though, and the expectations that the party's success aroused in its new adherents, created great difficulties for Brandt. It also produced a backlash among voters, particularly since left extremists in the Baader-Meinhof group, now reconstituted as the Red Army

Fraction, had taken to robbing banks and murdering judges. Brandt's proposal to encourage yet another manifestion of the left by offering concessions to Soviet Communism and by recognising its client regime in East Germany became even more alarming than it had been before. He had to find ways of reassuring people. One attempt was the proclamation of the so-called 'Radicals Edict' of January 1972, more usually known abroad as the *Berufsverbot* (bar to the professions), designed to exclude radicals from teaching and other public services. If Brandt's greatest achievement was the Ostpolitik (and the Deutschlandpolitik, as the part of it relating to *deutsch-deutsche* relations was more properly called), then his greatest mistake – or so he said himself – was this reactionary domestic counterpoise to it.

All politics is necessarily complex, since its essence is the practical resolution of differences of interest and outlook which are in principle irreconcilable. All human beings, too, are complex – but Brandt (like German politics) was perhaps more complex than most. He was certainly more complex than he seemed. In public there was something engagingly open and straightforward about him, even when he was at his most devious – something recognisably decent and human, to which many people in many different parts of the world responded. Even the new leftists were charmed by him. Even the personal assistant who was spying on him. His associates, though, often complained about the weaknesses he showed in private: his indecisiveness, his avoidance of confrontation, his uncommunicativeness, his proneness to depression, and his vanity. He made many conquests, but had few real friends. He extended a personal intimacy to a hall full of people, but not to many individuals taken on their own.

He *did* it, though; he achieved his great goal. This is the most difficult thing of all to understand about him. He performed that one single act that makes its mark upon the world, that defines and validates a life, and that eludes almost everybody.

*

With this play as with an earlier one of mine, *Copenhagen*, the question arises as to how much of it is fact and how much of it fiction. The division there, it seemed to me, was reasonably clear, since the characters were all shades returning from beyond the grave – and in any case almost every aspect of the real event that they were discussing was open to dispute. Even so I found myself being solemnly asked by probing interviewers if audiences might not be misled into thinking they were watching 'the truth'.

This play is open to more reasonable objections. The characters are all shown as being alive, the events in which they are participating as unfolding in the present tense. Very few of the words that these characters speak, however, were ever actually spoken by their real counterparts. What the feelings and ideas of those counterparts were, and whether the feelings and ideas expressed by my characters have anything in common with them, is a matter of interpretation and conjecture. The events themselves, and the world in which they take place, are hugely over-simplified. Any librarian should unhesitatingly file the play under fiction.

But, for anyone who is interested, this fiction does takes its rise from the historical record. All the political events referred to are real ones: the trips to Erfurt and Warsaw, the vanishing majority and the no-confidence vote, the triumph in the 1972 election and the gathering difficulties that followed it. The personalities of the protagonists are very much those attributed to their real counterparts by observers and historians. Brandt's drinking and womanising are not in dispute, nor are his 'feverish colds' and his taste for jokes. (Almost all the jokes that Brandt makes in the play are taken from a written collection he assembled.)[1] All the circumstances of his childhood that Brandt recalls, and all his adventures when he was operating underground in the

[1] For the reference to this and all other books mentiond in the Postscript, see the list of sources on page 129.

1930s for the Socialist Workers' Party, are taken from his memoirs and the standard biographies. The picture of life in the Palais Schaumburg, where the Federal Chancellor's office was housed, comes from various recorded accounts. So does that of life aboard the special train (which was indeed built for Reichsmarschall Göring, and which you can see now preserved in the historical museum in Bonn).

Two of the murkier topics touched upon in the play are factual. The first is the bribery that perhaps saved Brandt in the no-confidence vote. The truth about this began to come to light a year later, in the summer of 1973, when a CDU deputy called Julius Steiner confessed to having received 50,000 marks for withholding his vote against Brandt. He claimed that the money had come from Karl Wienand, the business manager of the Parliamentary SPD, who notoriously assisted Herbert Wehner in many of the shadier dealings on behalf of the Party for which Wehner enjoyed taking the credit. The money came from the Stasi, the East German Ministry of State Security.[1] Or so it is claimed in his memoirs by Markus Wolf, the legendary head of the Stasi's foreign intelligence service ('Mischa' to his colleagues, and said to be the model for John le Carré's Karla), and the allegation was accepted by the court that tried him in 1994, though Wienand, for what it's worth, denied it. The name of a second Christian Democrat deputy has since come to light in the Stasi files.

The other topic is the Federal Republic's secret ransoming of the Democratic Republic's political prisoners, and the equally secret payments it made to have people allowed out of East Germany to rejoin their families in the West. The DDR[2] carried on this cynical extortion at arm's

---

[1] More properly the MfS, the Ministerium für Staatssicherheit, which was responsible for both internal surveillance and for the foreign intelligence service. The latter, the HVA, the Hauptverwaltung Aufklärung (Chief Reconnaissance Directive), was the arm controlling Guillaume.

[2] Often known in English as the GDR, but this seems as awkward to me as it would be if in German the USA became the VSA.

length, through an East German lawyer called Wolfgang Vogel. When I stumbled across the trade in 1972 I was begged by officials of Amnesty International not to refer to it in the articles I was writing, for fear of jeopardising it. The income was so vast that it covered something like 20 per cent of the DDR's chronic balance-of-payments deficit in 'inter-German' trade. According to Vogel's own records, between 1964, when the trade started, and 1989, when the Wall came down, the Federal Republic bought out 33,755 prisoners and 215,019 people to be reunited with their families, at a total cost of 3,436 million Deutschmarks.

*

The most fictitious-looking aspect of the play is the role played by Günter Guillaume. Once again, though, I have followed the outline of the story fairly closely. His career in the Chancellor's office did begin almost simultaneously with Brandt's own. The doubts that were raised about his background were dismissed much as described in the play. Brandt did repeatedly ask his chief-of-staff Horst Ehmke (and later Günter Grabert, Ehmke's successor) to replace him; but somehow instead he did indeed get promoted from one position to another until, at the start of the 1972 election campaign, he took over as Brandt's personal assistant, with access to his files and in charge of organising the Chancellor's special train. On the train journeys he also accompanied Brandt as his valet, among other things, and was in charge of all his communications with Bonn and the rest of the world.

There are plenty of photographs of him, because he's in a lot of the pictures that were taken of Brandt. He's at the side of the room, or in the background, or walking a few paces behind the Chancellor, his hands folded respectfully behind his back, a dull, cosy, chubby figure in horn-rimmed spectacles and polite smile. He was known for his endless capacity for work and his equally endless good humour. He was always described as *kumpelhaft* (matey), a characteristic that was thought to be typically *berlinisch*. According to *Die Zeit*, he 'never lost the fried food smell of the Berlin *Hinterhof*'. A lot of the journalists around the Chancellor's office seem to have appreciated his easy-going chumminess. Brandt didn't; he found him servile. In some ways he was a kind of dim reflection of Brandt himself, with the same taste for the good life, and the same eye for women. Wibke Bruhns, a brilliant journalist on *Der Stern*, and one of the women with whom Brandt was said to have been involved, wrote memorably of Guillaume that he was 'nothing . . . a servant – not a person but a part of the place. You'd find him there just as you'd find a chair in the room.' Marianne Wichert-Quoirin, a local journalist who had known Guillaume at the time, described him to me as quite visibly the type of man that the DDR sent over – slightly old-fashioned and formal, given to wearing suits and buying flowers for ladies and helping them on with their coats.

His job as Brandt's assistant was a demanding one. The working day ended only when he laid out the last batch of papers on Brandt's night-table, and began again when he collected them first thing next morning, marked up with Brandt's annotations in green pencil. His few hours off each day must have been largely taken up with copying or photographing documents for his other employer. His home life was bleak. Wibke Bruhns caught the anonymity of the apartment where he and his wife Christel lived with her observation that it was furnished with the kind of potted plants that people give as presents; 'no one likes them, but no one throws them away.' Christel (somewhat too loud, sharp-tongued and rather charmless, according to Bruhns) was also a spy, and had been seen by their employers as the star until Günter had been so unexpectedly catapulted into the Chancellor's office. Their marriage was on the rocks. His only consolations were good lunches and dinners with his controller, an undetermined number of extra-marital liaisons, his teenage son Pierre, and the great secret that he nursed.

Apart from a conviction for drunk driving in 1972, there seems to be only one moment recorded when he showed any sign of the strain that he must have been living under.

This was on a trip he made with Brandt in the following
year to the South of France. Brandt was informed later,
according to his memoirs, that Guillaume had fallen asleep
after he had been drinking, and a notebook dropped out of
his pocket. When the security men accompanying the
Chancellor thoughtfully tried to put it back, Guillaume
awoke and mumbled: 'You swine! You won't catch me,
though!'

There were evidently more Günter Guillaumes than the
two who played out their simultaneous parts in the Palais
Schaumburg. When he finally appeared in court, the
summer after his arrest, a number of journalists noted the
change in his manner and appearance. *Der Spiegel* decided
that he had been underestimated. The new Guillaume, said
the magazine, was visibly endowed with 'judgement, vitality
and willpower'. He radiated, said the magazine, an
extraordinarily direct and intense warmth that made his
successes with women understandable. And in a long
television interview he gave much later, after he had been
released from prison and returned to the DDR, he has
changed once again. It's difficult to make any connection
between the pudgy little man in Bonn and the slim, bearded
figure on the television screen, whose alert dryness and
sharp tongue suggest the retired senior administrator rather
than the willing dogsbody.

All the aspects of the surveillance on Guillaume which
seem hardest to credit come from the record. Brandt was
indeed informed of the suspicions against his assistant and
sworn to silence. He was indeed encouraged to take
Guillaume off to Norway with him as his only assistant,
because Wilke and his deputy Schilling had holiday
arrangements of their own, and Guillaume was indeed
allowed to handle all the teleprinter traffic between Norway
and Bonn, unchecked and unobserved. Guillaume and his
wife did indeed throw a party for all the security staff. Also
taken from the record is the even more farcical confusion
between 'the second son' and 'the second man', and the
belatedness of its resolution.

*

About other details I have to sound a note of caution. The ticking of an unseen insect in the rafters of the Palais Schaumburg[1] and various other colourful touches are certainly taken from a published source. But the source in this case is Guillaume's own memoirs – and these have to be treated with a great deal of reserve.

They were ghosted, and first published in 1988 in the DDR – not for sale to the public but 'for official use only' (by the East German security services) – then reissued in the Federal Republic two years later. Markus Wolf, in *his* memoirs (also, of course, to be treated with circumspection), says that Guillaume's book was 'written in part to rub in the embarrassment of the affair to Bonn (after careful combing and adaptation by my service as disinformation – to protect other sources – and as positive PR for our work and its necessity)'.

Guillaume's book is curiously engaging, in spite of (or perhaps because of) its dubious provenance. But, some time between the collapse of the DDR in 1989 and his death in 1995, he gave a long interview to the journalist Guido Knopp, who was preparing a television programme about him, in which he cast even further doubt on it as a source. The ghost, he says, was 'a very nice journalist' supplied by the Stasi, who encouraged him to improve his stories somewhat. One of them, which had always puzzled me, about a meeting Guillaume claimed to have had in the Picasso Museum in Vallauris with 'a high-ranking man' in the intelligence service – presumably Wolf himself – he now disavowed completely. He also confessed to having built up the story of persuading Bauhaus to take the wrong dispatch-box back to Bonn at the end of the holiday in Norway. There were a whole series of boxes, he admitted, not just two, and he hadn't intended any deceit in getting Bauhaus to take one full of left-over souvenirs. I confess in my turn to

[1] Guillaume calls it a woodworm, but I'm informed by experts on infestation that if it knocked or ticked it must have been a death-watch beetle.

having kept to Guillaume's first version of the story, for the same reasons as he first told it.

Wolf in his memoirs is rather disparaging about Guillaume and his vanity, and he confesses frankly that he sees the downfall of Brandt through his agent's actitivities as 'the greatest defeat we suffered up to that time . . . equivalent to kicking a football into our own goal'. This may go some way to accounting for another discrepancy between Guillaume's book and the later interview. In the book Guillaume speaks about Wolf with the greatest warmth and respect. In the interview his tone has grown much sharper. 'Herr Wolf,' he says, 'shouldn't say things today that were not so. Just because it doesn't suit him in retrospect to accept responsibility. He was very quick to excuse himself before God and the world.'

Guillaume's attitude to his other employer, too, has become a little more critical. In the book he speaks of him with nothing but admiration (and his attitude was remarked upon at the time by Bruhns and others). Now he says that Brandt was not always easy to work with. He would much rather have been personal assistant to Helmut Schmidt, whom he regards as the Federal Republic's greatest Chancellor.

*

I have in any case exercised a good deal of licence in other directions, though I think this is in most cases fairly obvious. The continuous contact that my Guillaume has with his controller is plainly a dramatisation of their discrete monthly meetings. The conversations that Guillaume has with Brandt on the train go much further in this direction. In his memoirs Guillaume says that Brandt became another man on his travels: 'Other cities, other faces, other thoughts, other problems – he discovered a new impetus towards them. Suddenly he seemed free and relaxed . . . He became talkative, excited by every good joke . . . En route he tanked up, and I made it my business to give him as much chance as possible to do it.' When there were no election trips in

prospect, Guillaume invented the excuse of 'information
journeys' instead. He alleges that on their travels together
Brandt sometimes called him '*du*', and he felt obliged to
return the compliment. Nowhere, though, does he claim
that Brandt ever carried this intimacy as far as conversations
about his childhood or his personal feelings.

I have extended my licence even further in the case of the
holiday in Norway. The two families *were* together, and they
did have a certain amount of social contact. The story of the
relaxed mushrooming with Bauhaus, and of the games that
Matthias and Pierre played together in the woods, come
from Guillaume's memoirs. He says he was convinced that
Brandt had long since suppressed the memory of the
allegations against him – probably because he simply didn't
want to spoil the holiday. In the interview with Knopp,
however, a rather different picture emerges. Guillaume says
that Brandt was unusually silent with him in Norway, partly
because they both felt constrained by the presence of their
families. (Christel seems to have done most of the talking
when they were all together.) It is in any case unlikely that
Brandt had forgotten the allegations. Klaus Harpprecht,
Brandt's speechwriter, told Knopp that Brandt had made an
effort of his own before they left Bonn to get evidence
against Guillaume. He had 'touchingly' left threads on his
desk overnight, and carefully arranged files and pencils;
'he'd probably read about this in novels when he was a boy.'
His attempts in the play to sound Guillaume out while they
are in Norway by telling him about his own involvement in
underground activities before the war are my purely
invented equivalent to the threads and pencils (though what
Brandt recalls from those years is based very closely on what
he says himself in his memoirs).

I can only say that fact has subsequently outstripped any
fiction of mine in sheer implausibility. Brandt's son Matthias,
who is said to have played so happily in the Norwegian woods
with Guillaume's son Pierre, is now an actor. A German
television company has recently produced a dramatised
reconstruction of the case, and Matthias has entered the story
once again. Playing the part of Günter Guillaume.

*

Further licence with the narrative: I have made the
emergence of the Ostpolitik seem rather more clear-cut than
it was. Brandt had already been pursuing a policy of
rapprochement with the East as Foreign Minister in the Grand
Coalition. The desirability of improving relations with the
Soviet Union and its allies was a matter of general
agreement; the stumbling-block was the precondition for
this – acceptance of the Oder–Neisse frontier and
recognition of the DDR. What Brandt says on the subject in
the early stages of Act One is based closely upon various
speeches he made, but I'm not aware of any occasion where
he articulated it as completely as he does here, or where he
laid quite as much emphasis on it in a general context. In
later years he saw the Ostpolitik as his life's work, and
historians agree that it was the core programme and real
achievement of his government. But he knew only too well
how sensitive the subject was with a large proportion of the
voters, and in his declaration of the new government's
policy that followed the 1969 election he gave more
prominence to security, continuity and internal reform
('daring more democracy' – a famous phrase said to have
been contributed by Günter Grass). There are certain
parallels, one might think today, with the British
government's handling of entry into the European single
currency.

No one knows exactly what Brandt, Wehner and Schmidt
said to each other the night before the Chancellor's decision
to resign, and it notoriously happened not in Bonn but at a
party conference in the resort of Münstereifel; the name has
become part of SPD mythology, like Erfurt (where in 1891
the party adopted Marxism), and Bad Godesberg (where in
1959 it abandoned it). I have also shifted some actions from
offstage characters to onstage ones. According to
Guillaume's memoirs it was not Ehmke who gave
Guillaume his promotion to be Peter Reuschenbach's
replacement but Reuschenbach himself. Then again,
Bauhaus didn't volunteer his information about Guillaume's

knowledge of Brandt's womanising to Nollau personally but to his interrogators. The general absence of police and security men from the play is symptomatic of the staff shortages imposed by the economics of drama (both literal and metaphorical). Real politics is a labour-intensive business, and the Bundestag should have been teeming with deputies, the Palais Schaumburg with Ministers, advisers and civil servants – not to mention Germany as a whole with Germans.

For similar reasons I have sacked even a number of the principal protagonists in the story. The dismissal I regret most is that of Egon Bahr. Bahr was Brandt's closest confidant, a former radio journalist who had become his press representative back in the Berlin days. He was Brandt's trusted representative in the gruelling process of negotiating all the Eastern treaties (fifty meetings with the Russians alone). Brandt joked that Bahr didn't even know where France was, but he had a fascination with power politics and a natural bent for secret negotiation. Guillaume called him 'the sly fox', others 'Tricky Egon' (in English, presumably by analogy with the Tricky Dicky who was forced out of the White House three months after Brandt was out of the Palais Schaumburg).

He was an engaging and somewhat eccentric figure, who began his career as a pianist, but who was unable to pursue it in the Nazi period because one of his grandmothers was Jewish. In his retirement he took up one of the oddest hobbies I've ever heard of – travelling around the world with his wife as the only passengers aboard container ships, from one grim depot to another. When Wehner stood up in front of the party leadership after Brandt's resignation and talked about his love for Brandt's person and politics, Bahr put his hands over his face and wept. (Though it has to be said that this was on camera, and Karl Wienand remarked coldly that he'd seen Bahr weep before.) The dramatic problem is that, while he was away negotiating, his role in Bonn was more or less duplicated by Brandt's other confidant, Horst Ehmke, who coaxed Brandt out of his depressions (and got sidelined for his pains), and who as

116 Democracy

Brandt's chief of staff was much more closely involved in the
events surrounding Guillaume.

Also missing is another confidant of Brandt's, the
publisher Klaus Harpprecht, whom Brandt brought into his
second government as a speechwriter, and whose diary
supplies a lot of the atmosphere in the Palais Schaumburg
during those last eighteen months. I also wish I could have
found a way of introducing a most remarkable man who
made a marginal appearance earlier in *Copenhagen* – Georg
Duckwitz. In the 1940s, as the shipping specialist in the
German Embassy in Copenhagen, he had warned the
Danes exactly when the SS were to begin their round-up of
the Jews, which enabled almost all of them to be saved.
After the war he went back to Copenhagen as German
Ambassador, and was greatly honoured by the Danes,
before finishing his career as head of the Eastern
Department in the Foreign Office. Brandt was a personal
friend, and when he was still Foreign Minister in the Grand
Coalition brought him back from retirement, then as
Chancellor moved him to his personal staff to work on the
Ostpolitik.

The oddest economy of all, one may think, is the
exclusion of the entire female sex – particularly since it was
Brandt's relations with women that undid him. German
parliamentary politics at the time, though, was a man's
world; the story of Brandt's government might have been
rather different if it hadn't been so closed off from normal
demographic reality. There were a few women in the
Bundestag (and by the time Helmut Schmidt took office one
of them was President of it), but only one in the Cabinet. In
general, though, as was often noted, the only women whom
German politicians saw during the course of the working
week in Bonn were wives, secretaries and journalists, and
there are no women at all who are recorded as playing any
significant role in the arguments and struggles that form the
background to the play.

Two remarkable women stand on the fringes of it,
though, and there are other plays to be written about both
of them. One of them is Brandt's wife, Rut. He had been

married before during his time in Norway, and he married
for a third time in his late sixties. But for almost the whole of
his career his partner was Rut. She was a Norwegian who
had been involved in distributing material for the Resistance
during the German occupation, and he met her in
Stockholm in 1943. She was as attractive and charming as
her husband, the kind of wife that every traditional male
politician must dream of having at his side, and she behaved
with great dignity, generosity and humour throughout their
trials in 1974, and in their later divorce. The account she
gives in her memoirs of her escape as a girl from occupied
Norway, through the mountains into Sweden, is compelling;
so is her description of the devastation and misery that she
found in Berlin when she arrived with Willy at the end of
the war. By 1974 their marriage seems to have been
reduced more or less to a social arrangement, and during
the crisis she says that when Brandt was at home he went
around 'like a stranger in the house'. He subsequently
blamed her (along with Wehner) for his resignation, because
she had agreed with him that he should take responsibility
for the situation, and had made no attempt to dissuade him.

The other remarkable woman is Guillaume's wife,
Christel. She might have been created as Rut's antithesis –
cold, charmless and unapproachable. She was thought by
the journalists who met her to be much more intelligent
than her husband, and for a long time it was she who had
the starring role as a spy, because she had managed to get a
job in the Chancellery of Hesse, in Wiesbaden. She must
have had to make a painful readjustment when Guillaume
leapfrogged over her into the Federal Chancellery and she
was ordered to act as his courier – though by the time they
were both unmasked she seemed to be about to recover
some of the lost ground by getting a job in the Ministry of
Defence.

At no point, though, did she have much control over her
own destiny. She was not consulted about the Stasi's plan to
send her with her husband to the West – merely informed
about it and told to keep quiet and co-operate – while her
mother, who had Dutch nationality, was used as the lever

for getting permission for the three of them to settle in the
Federal Republic. She put on a great performance of
marital solidarity at their trial, because, she said much later,
she didn't want to appear weak. But the marriage had long
been dead, and kept in being only because the Stasi
required them to be a married couple. Many years later,
after the collapse of the DDR, she gave a long and
desolating television interview. Her life, she said, had been a
series of uprootings. She had been taken out of her own
country and dumped in the West to live a life of fiction.
Then dumped in prison, where she served over five years of
the eight to which she was sentenced, during which time she
lost contact with her son Pierre (another victim who could
step forward to claim a play about his own story). Then she
was dumped back in the DDR, and, as soon as her husband
was also exchanged and arrived to join her six months later,
dumped by him. Then dumped again, by the collapse of the
DDR, in yet another new and alien society. At the end of
the interview she sat in silence for some moments, thinking
back over it all. '*Ein verpfuschtes Leben*,' she said eventually –
'a botched life'.

*

There is a third, more shadowy, woman missing from the
play: Nora Kretschmann, the wife of Guillaume's controller.
But then my Arno Kretschmann himself is a simplification
of reality. At the beginning of his career in the Federal
Chancellery, Guillaume had other controllers whom he does
not name. In his interview with Guido Knopp, Guillaume
says that Kretschmann took over at the time of the election
campaign in the autumn of 1972. In his memoirs, though,
Guillaume dates his arrival a year earlier, and gives so many
circumstantial details that I suspect this version is more
likely to be the correct one. Although Kretschmann was
younger than him they seem to have hit it off immediately.
They had lunch together at their first meeting and found
themselves enjoying 'a conversation about God and the
world as completely unconstrained as any two men who

wanted to spend a stimulating afternoon with beer foam under their noses'. After this he remained controller until the Guillaumes were arrested.

It was proposed for a start that their meetings should take place in a secluded boat-house, but this meant that Guillaume would have to take up sailing, which he thought would be found to sort oddly with his known aversion to sporting activities, and in the end they agreed to meet quite openly in and around Bonn. So openly, in fact, that Kretschmann would occasionally come to the Chancellery and have Guillaume summoned on the house phone. But usually they met in restaurants and bars, often for convivial evenings with their wives present. Guillaume says that Christel and Nora got on well together, and if this is true then these occasions must have been one of the brighter spots in his wife's bleak life.

The Kretschmanns had been fictionalised long before I got near them. They were a married couple, names unknown, who had been sent separately to the West, as 'Franz Tondera' and 'Sieglinde Fichte', and they had begun by establishing separate and very different cover stories. According to Guillaume in his memoirs, Franz travelled for a well-known firm in the motor industry (he doesn't say which), while Sieglinde, having given up her training as a vet in the DDR, worked on a factory production line with Turkish and Greek women guest-workers. They were then directed to make each other's acquaintance by chance on a ski-ing course, fall in love, conduct a bashful courtship and get married all over again. So now Sieglinde Fichte of Ulm, otherwise Ursula Behr of Stuttgart, was Sieglinde Tondera of Cologne. Except that the Tonderas for some reason became Arno and Nora Kretschmann (their given names were extracted, according to the *Spiegel*, from a rearrangement of letters in 'Tondera'.) When the Guillaumes were arrested, the Kretschmanns, in all their shifting avatars, vanished, and even the most diligent searches since the collapse of the DDR in the files of the Stasi, the source of so many revelations about so many people, have so far uncovered no trace of them.

*

A number of other questions about the case remain
unanswered. Exactly what information, for a start, did
Guillaume pass on? He preferred to report to his controller
orally, and his information – certainly before the election
campaign of 1972, when he first had access to documents –
came by his own account chiefly from office gossip. Files
and notes, Brandt is reported to have said when he gave
evidence at the Guillaumes' trial,[1] were much less important
than the insights he could have got from informal functions.
Various journalists covering the case filled in the likely
circumstances.

> Lunch with a Minister President, coffee with a city mayor
> – on such occasions not every word is carefully weighed.
> What relations do leading politicians have to one
> another . . . ? When, for example, after a session at a
> Party conference, Schmidt, Wehner, and Brandt visited a
> *Weinstube* and went on talking – Guillaume would be at
> the next table . . . In the car after long sessions of the
> Party Executive, when Brandt gave vent to 'expressions of
> displeasure', or 'characterised' somebody . . . When the
> SPD chiefs talked over a cup of coffee or – at the end of
> the day – over something stronger, about who was going
> to be renominated or not and where . . . He could catch
> the nuances of what was said, and hear confidential
> briefings to journalists on matters that might later make
> the headlines. He knew much more than any state secret
> – he knew about the moods, connections, and
> developments that could lead to the decisions taken later.

As Bahr said in evidence: 'He was always there, but

[1] Any account of the case has to rely heavily upon press reports (often
remarkably divergent) because in German law there is no such thing as
an official transcript of the proceedings, only a summary of the evidence
made by the court as part of its judgement.

people weren't aware of him.' Wilke recalled him as always wanting to be in on everything, whether it concerned him or not. Guillaume himself said in his interview with Knopp that he couldn't remember what he'd passed on, but agreed that it included everything he could lay his hands on about the negotiations with Moscow and East Berlin. Stephan Konopatzky, a researcher working on the Stasi files now held in a massive archive in Berlin, can find relatively little information credited to XV/19142/60 and XV/11694/60, aka Hansen and Heinze, aka Günter and Christel Guillaume, and less still that was regarded as of any great value. He concedes that Guillaume's reports may, because of their importance and sensitivity, have been handled by some special channel as yet unexplored in the archive, but thinks it more likely that he was being used very cautiously to protect his unique position. When one thinks of all those monthly debriefings by Arno aka Franz, though . . . What happened to everything that was said? Was it the supportive Arno who thought it wasn't worth passing on?

    If Wolf is telling the truth in his memoirs he must have received much more material than the files reveal. He says that before Brandt's visit to Erfurt in March 1970 – i.e., even at the very beginning of Guillaume's employment in the Chancellor's office, when he was still concerned with nothing more than trade union liaison – he 'gained access to some of the West German plans, which, combined with information from other sources, gave us a clearer idea of Brandt's intentions and fears'. He also says that Guillaume's 'real importance for us in East Berlin lay in his political instincts. Through Guillaume's judgements we were able to conclude sooner rather than later that Brandt's new Ostpolitik, while still riven with contradictions, marked a genuine change of course in West German foreign policy. As such, his work actually aided détente by giving us the confidence to place our trust in the intentions of Brandt and his allies.'

    There is a further striking discrepancy between the files and Wolf's account. The files contain nothing about Brandt's extra-marital affairs. In his memoirs, though, Wolf claims to know that 'Guillaume soon realised that Brandt's adultery was frequent and varied'. Then again, after Guillaume was unmasked, and the head of the Federal Criminal Police wrote his report on Brandt's private life, cataloguing what Wolf calls 'his affairs with journalists, casual acquaintances, and prostitutes', he claims that 'Guillaume had of course been telling us about this kind of behavior all along'. So perhaps the surviving files don't record the whole story.

The range of material on which the court case was based was narrow. The charge brought against the Guillaumes was the most serious possible: '*schwerer Landesverrat*' – high treason. It would have been impossible to secure a conviction on this merely for passing on gossip and unspecified overheard remarks – or even documents, if no one knew what the documents were. So the case depended largely upon Guillaume's spontaneous admission at the moment of his arrest to being an 'officer' of the DDR, and also upon the only specific documents that he was known for certain to have handled – the teleprinter traffic on the Norwegian holiday.

There remains some doubt, however, as to whether any of this material ever reached East Berlin. In his memoirs Guillaume says that he didn't attempt to contact his controller during the holiday, but gives a very graphic and circumstantial account of how he arranged for the copies of all the documents in his possession to be photographed by a courier while he was making an overnight stop at a hotel in Sweden on the way back to Bonn. In the interview with Knopp, as we have seen, he withdraws his claim to have deliberately fooled Bauhaus into thinking that he was carrying the documents himself, but doesn't modify any other part of the story. All this is cast into doubt by Markus Wolf's memoirs, however. Wolf says that the copies were handed over by Christel to a courier called Anita at the Casselsruhe restaurant in Bonn, and that Anita, realising she was being followed, threw them into the Rhine. So he never received them, though he kept this fact from Guillaume so as not to hurt his pride. Konopatzky agrees that there is no trace of any of the Norwegian messages in the files.

Oddly, though, Wolf makes no reference at all to Guillaume's version of the handover, by way of the courier in the Swedish hotel. Even more oddly, perhaps, he recounts in some detail the contents of the three most important messages that Guillaume copied, but doesn't explain where the information came from; not from the Guillaumes' trial, plainly, where the evidence relating to this was given in camera. More oddly still, in a television interview with Guido Knopp for his programme on Guillaume, he says that the documents in the dispatch-box *did* reach East Berlin, though he refuses to say what happened to them.

The story of Christel's meeting at the Casselsruhe restaurant, incidentally, is recounted in Guillaume's book. As in Wolf's version, her lunch companion realised she was being kept under observation, and found herself being tailed when she left the restaurant. Guillaume, who calls the woman not Anita but Thomin, purports to be much amused by his interrogators' suspicion later that she had been a courier. She thought, he says, that the watchers were private detectives employed by her husband because she was having an affair.

*

There are a number of other points of dispute in the record, where I have had to choose one version or another. According to Brandt's notes on the case (see the list of Brandt's writings on page 130), his bodyguard Ulrich Bauhaus came to him 'with tears in his eyes' and assured him that he had given his interrogators information about Brandt's women only under pressure; he was astonished at how much had already been collected. In a television interview much later, however, Karl Wienand says that Bauhaus went voluntarily to offer his evidence, because he and the other security people, as ordinary citizens in bowler hats and umbrellas, were

genuinely shocked by the Chancellor's behaviour. Neither
Wienand's record nor his appearance incline one to place
much confidence in anything he says, but *someone* must
have first brought up the question of the women, and of
Guillaume's awarenesss of them, and I have followed
Wienand's version.

I have also given expression to some of the many
conspiracy theories that have been aired. Most of them have
centred on the role played by Herbert Wehner, the
Chairman of the Parliamentary Party of the SPD and its
éminence grise. There is general agreement that Wehner was a
Machiavellian figure, and relations between him and Brandt
had always been difficult; even during the Grand Coalition
they had been reduced to communicating through an
intermediary. Brandt's single-handed 'cavalry charge' to the
Chancellorship in 1969 was perhaps, among other things, a
declaration of independence fromWehner, and in no way
improved Wehner's low assessment of Brandt's suitability
for the job. He thought Brandt a lightweight. The publisher
Rudolf Augstein once overheard him saying that Brandt
and Walter Scheel (the Foreign Minister and leader of the
FDP, therefore Brandt's coalition partner – another central
character missing from the play) were both gigolos – '*Sie
können nicht regieren, sondern erigieren*' ('Their forte is not so
much government as erection'). Wehner went to quite
extraordinary lengths to undermine Brandt during his
second term, and to prepare the way for Helmut Schmidt to
succeed him. But, only a few weeks before Brandt's
resignation, when Schmidt at last made an open bid for the
Chancellorship, Wehner seems to have had a sudden
belated realisation of how much he needed Brandt's appeal
to both voters and party members, and the two men had a
bizarre *rapprochement* (which I reluctantly cut out of the play
as one complication too many) – a long meeting at Brandt's
home, with many pauses for thoughtful silence and the
consumption of red wine, conspiring together against
Schmidt.

This odd turn of events, however, did nothing to allay the
suspicions of both Brandt and the press later that Wehner

had played some kind of underhand role in the Chancellor's resignation. The version in the press was that Wehner had conspired in one way or another with his protégé, Günther Nollau, the President of the Federal Office for the Protection of the Constitution (the counter-espionage service). It was suggested that in 1973 Nollau had informed Wehner of the suspicions against Guillaume before he told Hans-Dietrich Genscher, the Minister of the Interior, to whom he was formally responsible. Nollau always vehemently denied this. He insisted that he had told Genscher on 29 May, and Wehner not until 4 June. He remembered the latter date very clearly, he said, because it was his own birthday. Genscher, however, seems a little sceptical of this in his memoirs. 'What did worry me,' he says, 'was that Nollau kept Wehner informed of the investigation. What would Wehner do with this knowledge, since as everyone knew, he was increasingly critical of Willy Brandt's chancellorship?' Arnulf Baring, the standard historian of the period, is inclined to agree. Nollau's forewarning of Wehner, which might have been on 23 May, the very day that the file landed on Nollau's desk, he finds 'exceedingly likely'.

Genscher didn't like Nollau, and blamed him afterwards for telling untruths about the amount of information he had passed on about the case. His behaviour, he said, 'confirmed many of the prejudices raised against him previously'. Brandt didn't like him, either, and refers to him sarcastically in his memoirs as 'supposedly able'. Nollau certainly pursued the case with remarkable ineptitude and desuetude, if nothing worse. His appearance in subsequent television interviews inclines one to share all the prejudices and suspicions that were expressed against him; just as well, you feel, as with Wienand, that he was not in the second-hand car trade, or he might not have got as far as he did.

Guillaume also came to believe that there was a conspiracy – but in his version Wehner, Nollau and Genscher were all in it together. Nollau, he is reported to have said in the evidence he gave when his old employer

Markus Wolf was in his turn tried for treason in 1933,[1] was the confidant of Genscher as well as of Wehner, and both of them wanted to force Brandt out. 'Nollau held out the knife, and Genscher gave Brandt the necessary push to make him run on to it.' He himself, he said, in a slightly different version of the metaphor, had been used as the club with which Brandt had been struck.

Brandt himself was obsessed with suspicions of a rather different conspiracy against him – between Herbert Wehner and the East German leadership. He recorded them in a series of cryptic notes, written at some point after his retirement but not published until 1994, and held to them for the rest of his life. They centred on Wehner's known contacts in East Berlin. Wehner reported to Brandt two meetings there. The first was with Erich Honecker, the East German party leader, and its purpose, according to Wehner, was to relaunch the secret trade in political prisoners and family reunions, which had ironically been brought to an end by the regularisation of relations between the two states in the newly signed Basic Treaty. The second was with Wolfgang Vogel, the middleman in this trade, though the subject in this case was said by Wehner to be economic collaboration in general. The timing of both meetings was unsettling – the first on the evening of 29 May 1973, the day that Nollau told Genscher, and Genscher told Brandt, about the suspicions against Guillaume, and the second on 3 May 1974, the day that Nollau told Wehner about the list of Brandt's women. In any case Brandt believed that Wehner had had additional contacts with East

[1] Wolf was convicted, but two years later the judgement was overturned by the Federal Constitutional Court, which ruled that former officers of the DDR intelligence service could not be prosecuted for treason and espionage. Whether he was at all grateful for this expression of the rule of law, or even amused by the irony of it, in the Federal Germany of which he now found himself a citizen, and which he had worked so hard and so skilfully to undermine, he does not say in his memoirs. Brandt, incidentally, was one of the people who had spoken out against his prosecution in the first place.

Berlin which had gone unreported. In the course of them, he suspected, Wehner had been told that Guillaume was a spy, and had also been primed to launch his extraordinary attack on him from Moscow in the autumn of 1973.

Brandt's information was provided by Egon Bahr, who had obtained it from the Russians. It had come by way of the secret system of communication that Bahr had established with the Soviet leader Leonid Brezhnev, in imitation of the 'back-channels' used by Henry Kissinger to negotiate with the Soviet Union. The historian August H. Leugers-Scherzberg has recently cast more light on this dark corridor, and the allegations against Wehner that it was used to convey. What neither Bahr nor Brandt realised, says Dr Scherzberg, is that the chain of communication led through Yuri Andropov, later Brezhnev's successor, but at that time head of the KGB. Andropov had reasons to want Wehner discredited in Brandt's eyes, because Wehner distrusted the 'back-channel', and wanted to replace it with a more direct link, while Andropov himself naturally wished to preserve it as an instrument for his own influence. Wehner also dissented from Brandt's belief that an understanding with the Soviet Union was the key that would unlock relations with East Germany, and wanted to distribute the Federal Republic's efforts at reconciliation more broadly around Eastern Europe.

Whatever Wehner did or didn't do behind the scenes, however, his assurance of support for Brandt at the crucial moment in Münsteifel seems to have been less than whole-hearted, and Brandt always held him responsible (together with Rut) for failing to dissuade him from a decision that he never ceased to regret.

*

I've had much help with this project. First of all (once again) from Sarah Haffner, who got me off on the right foot as soon as I told her what I had in mind, by recommending me to read Arnulf Baring's *Machtwechsel*, and who subsequently supplied me with further parcels of books and help in

translating a number of particularly awkward phrases. Peter
Merseburger, the political journalist, who was working in
Bonn during the Brandt Chancellorship and whose own
biography of Brandt has since appeared, gave me a great
deal of patient advice. He also introduced me to Klaus
Harpprecht, Brandt's speechwriter, and asked his old
colleague Fritz Pleitgen to open the film archives of
Westdeutscher Rundfunk in Cologne for me.

Eva Giesel, a colleague of my German play agent Ursula
Pegler, spent much time, energy and ingenuity making
contacts and inquiries on my behalf. I originally expected
the play to lay more emphasis on the Guillaumes' trial, and
Frau Giesel worked particularly hard at putting me in touch
with officials of the court where it took place, the
Oberlandesgericht in Düsseldorf. My thanks, too, to Herr
Bundesanswalt Lampe, in the office of the
Generalbundesanwalt in Karlsruhe, who explained some of
the basics of German law to me, and to Professor Peter
Brandt, Willy Brandt's eldest son, who most kindly offered
to see me, though in the end I decided it might inhibit me;
to Frau Gertrud Lenz in the Friedrich-Ebert-Stiftung in Bad
Godesberg, where the Brandt papers are lodged; to Fritz
Pleitgen at WDR; to ZDF for the text of Guido Knopp's
interview with Guillaume; to Frau Marianne Wichert-
Quoirin, who covered Federal politics in Bonn and the
Guillaume trial in Düsseldorf for the *Kölner Stadt-Anzeiger*;
and to Finn Aaserud for the Norwegian.

The amount of material available turned out to be
oceanic, and for the first time in my life, when I finally had
to recognise that I was drowning, I got the help of a
research assistant. My choice – Stefan Kroner, the
dramaturg who had worked on one of the German
productions of *Copenhagen* – turned out to be inspired. He
was not only unbelievably quick and industrious, but had an
uncanny ability to guess what I should find useful. He
plunged into the archive of the Friedrich-Ebert-Stiftung,
and of WDR in Cologne, and reduced the tons of press-
cuttings and weeks of newsreel to proportions I could just
about manage. He found books long out of print, and

trawled information from the huge deposits of old Stasi files in Berlin (still not fully explored, and a rich potential source of fossil fuel). We also had a delightful trip around the Rhineland together, to see where it all happened and to visit the various archives.

*

For anyone interested in finding out more about the case itself, or the personalities and politics of the period, the following is a short list of the more easily available material:

General

Baring, Arnulf: *Machtwechsel, die Ära Brandt-Scheel* (1983, 1998). The standard history of the period. Long (nearly a thousand pages), but boldly and incisively written. The chapters on the Guillaume affair and Brandt's resignation are relatively brief and particularly fine.

Harpprecht, Klaus: *Im Kanzleramt: Tagebuch der Jahre mit Willy Brandt* (2000). Harpprecht is a well-known publisher who joined Brandt's office at the beginning of 1973 as a speech-writer and adviser. He was also a personal friend of Brandt's, and provided him with a holiday house in the South of France which gave him some respite from the political storms of that difficult year. His diary of life in the Palais Schaumburg is sharp, worldly and observant – and a salutary corrective to the schematic oversimplification of my picture.

Rehlinger, Ludwig A.: *Freikauf* (1991). For the rate of ransom per prisoner charged by the DDR.

Whitney, Craig R.: *Advocatus Diaboli: Wolfgang Vogel – Anwalt zwischen Ost und West* (1993). For the complete figures of the trade in prisoners and family reunions, as given in Vogel's own files.

Brandt's own writings

Brandt, Willy: *Erinnerungen* (1989). The 1994 edition also contains the *Notizen zum Fall G*, the notes about the Guillaume affair that he made around the time of his resignation. There is an English edition, *My Life in Politics* (1992), but it doesn't include the *Notizen*.

A complete collection of Brandt's works is in the course of publication (the *Berliner Ausgabe*). The volume relating to the domestic and social policy of his government is Volume 7, *Mehr Demokratie wagen: Innen- und Gesellschaftspolitik 1966–1974* (2001). The volume relating to his government's foreign policy (including relations with East Germany) is Volume 6, *Ein Volk der guten Nachbarn, Außen- und Deutschlandpolitik 1966–1974*. This has not yet appeared, however, and for his speeches and other statements on foreign policy I have used:

Brandt, Willy: *Reden und Interviews 1968–1969* (German government publication, undated), and *Bundeskanzler Brandt: Reden und Interviews* (1971).

Brandt, Willy: *Lachen hilft – Politische Witze* (2001). A collection of jokes, mostly but not exclusively political, assembled by Brandt over the course of the years. It was completed and published after his death by his widow, Brigitte Seebacher-Brandt. This is the source of most of Brandt's jokes in the play.

Biographies of Brandt

Merseburger, Peter: *Willy Brandt 1913–1992, Visionär und Realist* (2002). The most recent. Well-written and comprehensive, unashamedly partisan, with a foreword that gives a particularly brilliant overview of Brandt's achievements.

Koch, Peter: *Willy Brandt* (1998). Colourful, journalistic, gossipy, and highly readable.

Marshall, Barbara: *Willy Brandt, a Political Biography*. In English. Short but to the point.

Schöllgen, Gregor: *Willy Brandt – die Biographie* (2001). Compact and serviceable.

Guillaume

Guillaume, Günter: *Die Aussage*. The original edition, described as *'protokolliert von Günter Karau'*, was published by the East German military publishing-house in 1988 for the benefit of the security organs and the National People's Army, marked 'for official use only'. In 1990 it was reissued in West Germany in a revised form, as *Die Aussage – wie es wirklich war* ('The Testimony – how it really was'; the implication is presumably that the book is a substitute for the testimony which Guillaume refused to give at his trial). For the reserve with which this source should be treated see above. It should really be read in conjunction with:

Knopp, Guido: *Top Spione* (1997), and the TV programme that this was published in association with (ZDF 1994); or, better still, the transcript of the interview conducted with Guillaume by Knopp and Steinhauser that was obtained for me from ZDF (TV2) by Stefan Kroner, though this seems not to have been published. It appears to be the full text of a conversation from which only excerpts have been used in the programme itself, though it has no date or other indication of its provenance.

The assessment of Guillaume's reports as it appears in the files of the Stasi comes from a contribution by Stephan Konopatzky to a conference on the role of the Stasi in the West, in November 2001, organised under the auspices of the organisation that now holds the archive, the office of *Die Bundesbeauftragte für die Unterlagen des Staatssicherheitsdienstes der ehemaligen DDR* (the Federal Commissioners for the Documents of the State Security Service of the Former DDR).

Other characters in the story

Wolf, Markus (with Anna McElvoy): *Man Without a Face* (1997). His memoirs, in English. Very lively and absorbing, and apparently frank about many things, though reserving the right to silence on others.

Genscher, Hans-Dietrich: *Erinnerungen* (1995). Memoirs. In English as *Rebuilding a House Divided* (1995).

Brandt, Rut: *Freundesland* (1992). Her memoirs, and as engaging as Frau Brandt herself.

Schmidt, Helmut: *Weggefährten* (1996). Memoirs.

Leugers-Scherzberg, August H.: *Die Wandlungen des Herbert Wehner, von der Volksfront zur Großen Koalition* (2002). This is the standard biography of Herbert Wehner, but it takes him only as far as the Grand Coalition. Until the next volume appears:

Leugers-Scherzberg, August H.: *Herbert Wehner und der Rücktritt Willy Brandts am 7. Mai 1974* (in the *Vierteljahreshefte für Zeitgeschichte*, Part 2, April 2002).

Nollau, Günther: *Das Amt* (1982) Memoirs. Relevant extracts in *Der Stern* (11 September 1975).

Ehmke, Horst: *Mittendrin* (1994). Memoirs.

Bahr, Egon: *Zu meiner Zeit* (1996). Memoirs.